What People Are Saying About
The Motherhood Club . . .

"There is a moment of panic a new mother faces when the baby is fed and diapered but still crying like there is something wrong. This is the time when a woman faces her inexperience and thinks *I can't do this!* In this enormously helpful book, Shirley Washington recognizes this moment happens to all new mothers and offers a humorous, kind and understanding look at how new mothers learn to be good mothers. I would recommend this book to any expectant woman getting ready for her first child."

—Melinda L. Surbaugh
managing editor, *Today's Dallas Woman*

"A mom's feelings and special needs are too often overlooked during the joy of birth when everyone's looking after baby. *The Motherhood Club* is an uplifting and comforting guide to help us through the emotional challenges, while ensuring us we are not alone."

—Tory Johnson
CEO of Women for Hire and mother of
four-year-old twins

"*The Motherhood Club* is the perfect resource for any expectant or new mom who is looking for inspiration and around-the-clock support. Shirley Washington and the members of the club offer candid advice and insights into motherhood, and will help any mom looking for tips and parenting know-how. I highly recommend every new mother run out and buy this book today!"

—Robyn Freedman Spizman
coauthor, *Getting Through to Your Kids*

THE MOTHERHOOD CLUB

Help, Hope and Inspiration
for New Mothers from
New Mothers

Shirley Washington
and
Ann Dunnewold, Ph.D.

Health Communications, Inc.
Deerfield Beach, Florida

www.hci-online.com

This publication is designed to provide accurate and authoritative information with regard to the subject matter covered. It is sold with the understanding that the publisher and/or authors are not engaged in rendering psychological, medical or other professional services. If expert assistance or counseling is needed, the services of a competent professional should be sought.

Library of Congress Cataloging-in-Publication Data

The Motherhood Club : help, hope, and inspiration for new mothers from new mothers / [compiled by] Shirley Washington and Ann Dunnewold.
    p. cm.
    Includes bibliographical references.
    ISBN 0-7573-0002-2 (tradepaper)
    1. Motherhood. 2. Mothers—Case studies. 3. Mother and infant—Case studies. I. Washington, Shirley, 1962- II. Dunnewold, Ann. III. Series.

HQ759 .M8739 2002
306.874'3—dc21

2002190210

Publisher: Health Communications, Inc.
    3201 S.W. 15th Street
    Deerfield Beach, FL 33442-8190

Cover design by Andrea Perrine Brower
Inside book design by Lawna Patterson Oldfield

To Mothers

The Motherhood Club Creed

I do solemnly swear that I will be the best mother I can
possibly be.

I will love, feed, hold, clothe, rock, shelter, protect and
nurture my baby.

I will question other mothers about basic baby care issues I
don't understand.

I will question other mothers about emotions I don't
understand.

I will question other mothers about mothering issues I don't
understand.

I will not label myself a bad mother.

I will not wrap myself in a blanket of guilt.

I will not be afraid to admit I love my baby, but feel
overwhelmed with mothering.

I will not take myself too seriously.

I will not surrender to fear.

I will take control.

I will trust my instincts.

I will believe in me.

I will take time to laugh.

I will take mommy moments.

I will love myself.

I will enjoy the splendor of motherhood.

I will be the best mother I can possibly be!

—SHIRLEY WASHINGTON

Contents

Foreword

If you ask a woman what one experience most changed her life, she'll probably answer "becoming a mother." Whether through adoption or birth, motherhood is a life-changing event that forever alters how you define yourself and how you see the world around you. Once you hold *your* child in your arms you can never go back to the way you were.

While these changes define and enrich us, the road to motherhood is often complex and challenging and can make even the most confident woman feel inadequate and helpless. New mothers, especially, find themselves in uncharted territory trying to speak a whole new language. Through the veil of mind-numbing sleep deprivation they must interpret their baby's unrelenting cries. Does she need sleep, food, a dry diaper? Is he in pain or does he just want to be held?

With the birth of my first grandson, I witnessed firsthand how motherhood could take an otherwise very competent and accomplished young professional woman and turn her into a self-doubting, insecure and very stressed new mother. The new role was the most difficult she had ever played, and with next to no training to rely on, it was no wonder she was a frightened bundle of nerves. Fortunately for my daughter, Andrea, nurturance and a new sense of confidence quickly replaced this period of self-doubt. But this is not always the case for new mothers, especially when family members are not available, and support systems are not firmly in place.

Aside from all the new responsibilities of motherhood, most women are unprepared for the feelings of loneliness they often experience. After all the hubbub of preparing for the birth of the baby, they are suddenly left by themselves with a little one whose daily activities center around but a few activities: crying, sleeping and soiling their diapers. The loads of laundry seem to have no end and the four walls offer a poor substitute for adult conversation.

In our mobile society, many women are miles away from the love and support of their families. While Grandma might come for a short visit at first, most women don't have the advantage of having their mothers drop by to show them how to comfort their inconsolable child or to baby-sit while they catch up on their sleep after being up all night.

Even women lucky enough to have their mother in the same city might find that she just doesn't understand the new way of raising children. Babies must now sleep on their backs, not their tummies; baby powder is a no-no for newborns; it's okay to rush to a crying baby without fear of "spoiling" him; little ones learning to walk will best gain this new skill barefoot than with stiff white shoes. There are so many changes and differing philosophies.

Many times on my show I have seen women so over-whelmed with their new responsibilities that they were near the breaking point. Some new mothers were still children themselves, while others had neither the financial ability nor the emotional stability to enter into motherhood. Yet, prepared or not, they were new mothers with awesome responsibilities that had to be met. But the majority of new mothers I meet are just like you, happy to be starting a new family. And they too, are so overwhelmed, that they are near the breaking point. While some bond with their babies immediately, others take a while to warm up to the relationship. They feel they aren't cut out to be mothers, that they must be missing a "mothering gene." Other women are troubled by the lack of support their husbands have for their new role of "mother." Exhausted from trying to take care of their babies, new mothers certainly don't have the time or energy to go back to being the "care-free wife" their husbands want.

Then there's the frightening issue of postpartum depression. Hormones affect every person differently. Sometimes women are leveled with an overwhelming sadness that they don't understand and from which they cannot escape without help. We have seen how not paying attention to these signs can have tragic consequences.

My daughter's journey into motherhood reminded me of how important it is to share our experiences with others in the same situation. As Andrea reached out to other new mothers who were dealing with the same issues of self-doubt and worry, she found that she was not alone. And in numbers there is not just safety, but security and growth. Sharing fears with one another, Andrea and her new friends became stronger and more relaxed mothers. And I returned to being the mother of a confident and radiant daughter, who had blessed me with a much loved and well-cared-for grandson, Max.

What most new mothers need is a support group where they can share their experiences with other women who are going through the same things they are. Only another new mom can understand how you can have been awake since five o'clock but don't have time to comb your hair until noon; how bone-tired getting up three times a night can make you; how removed you feel from your old life; how you long for an afternoon off but can't stand the thought of leaving your baby even for a minute.

The Motherhood Club is that support group—and more. In this wonderful book, Shirley Washington and Ann Dunnewold introduce you to new moms just like yourself. They are women who, pre-baby, were capable and articulate, ready to take on any challenge handed them. Now, with baby at home in the newly decorated nursery, they feel scared and helpless. Their candid descriptions about life with a baby will make you nod your head in agreement and convince you that you are not alone. Together with the club members you will learn the many myths of new motherhood and discover that you do not have to be—that, indeed, you cannot be—a superwoman.

You'll learn savvy strategies to make new motherhood easier. You'll learn to relax and enjoy your new role—the most important you will ever have. In fact, you'll feel so good about motherhood, you'll want to have another baby just to experience the wonder all over again. Andrea just did, making me the proud grandmother of both Max and his baby brother Kyle.

Welcome to *The Motherhood Club* and good luck as you discover the innumerable joys that await you.

—*Sally Jessy Raphael*

Acknowledgments

When I first started interviewing mothers for *The Motherhood Club*, I did not realize how much I would be touched by their moving stories. I felt very close and connected to them. That was very special to me. These courageous mothers came forward without a hint of hesitation to share their stories. And they spoke openly and candidly about an immensely personal part of their lives in an effort to help other mothers. For that, I am truly grateful and express my deepest appreciation to each of them.

There were so many people who helped me in my search for first-time mothers to interview for *The Motherhood Club* and I am thankful for their assistance: Lori Allen at *Lifetime Live;* Rae Cox, vice-president Mid-Cities Mothers of Multiples; Marty Otero-Esquivel, public relations officer with The National Society of Hispanic MBAs; David Starr, producer of *The Tom Joyner Morning Show*; Eric Wesley, media relations officer at Parkland Memorial Hospital in Dallas; and Jean Carpenter, Melissa Jue, Audrey Keymer, Dorothy McClerking, Dana Rogers and Christine Volkner. Thank you all.

I received a lot of encouragement from family and friends while writing *The Motherhood Club*. I am extremely grateful to my husband and son for their eternal love, unwavering support and never-ending patience, and for making me a proud member of the Motherhood Club. Thank you. I love you to infinity and beyond! I would also like to thank my parents for their love, encouragement and guidance. A very special thank you to my mother-in-law for giving so much of "you" to help "me." To my grandparents, mother-in-law, siblings, nieces, nephews, cousins and friends—thank you for loving and supporting me. I love you all from the bottom of my heart. Deep felt thanks to my great-grandmothers for teaching me to look beyond the "X." I can feel your smiles from heaven. With great gratitude I would also like to thank Emma Rogers, co-owner of Black Images Book Bazaar in Dallas, for your wisdom and sound advice. I appreciate you!

A very special thank you to Dr. Ann Dunnewold, for your time, commitment and invaluable contribution to *The Motherhood Club*. You're the best! A Texas-size thank you to my agent, David Hale Smith. A very special thank you to Peter Vegso, the publisher at Health Communications, Inc., and his staff for working wholeheartedly on *The Motherhood Club:* Allison Janse, Kathy Grant, Lawna Patterson Oldfield, Dawn Grove, Larissa Hise, Maria Dinoia, Kim Weiss, Kelly

Maragni, Randee Feldman, Terry Burke, Irena Xanthos and Lori Golden. And finally, an extra special thank you to a very special mother, who recognized the value of *The Motherhood Club* and fully understood its mission at conception: Christine Belleris, editorial director at Health Communications, Inc. Thank you for your insight, support and guidance. And especially for helping me deliver *The Motherhood Club*!

And last, but certainly not least, thank you for reading *The Motherhood Club*. I hope you find encouragement and comfort within its pages.

—Shirley Washington

Thanks, first of all, to all the mothers in my life: my own mother and grandmothers, my sisters, friends and clients. Knowing you and watching you in action has expanded my knowledge of this wondrous experience. And thanks also to my daughters and husband, without whom I would not have had induction into The Motherhood Club.

Thanks to my dear friend Shirley Smith Duke, who proofed and encouraged me along the writer's way, for this work and others. And thanks to my dear friend Cynthia Curry, Ph.D., who ceaselessly lauds my expertise and success.

Special thanks to Christine Belleris and everyone else at Health Communications, Inc., for your supportive and expert work on this book. I am truly impressed with your commitment and professionalism.

A heartfelt thanks to Shirley Washington for finding me,

believing in the value of my knowledge and perspective on this project, and making it possible for me to contribute to this work.

—*Ann Dunnewold, Ph.D.*

Introduction

Welcome to the Motherhood Club! It is an exclusive club that welcomes all women who have received the most precious, most exquisite gift ever: a baby. Because of your special bundle of joy, you have entered into the sanctity of motherhood and have earned the coveted and endearing title: Mother. You will wear that label proudly—like a badge of honor—because becoming a mother is the most beautiful, fulfilling and rewarding experience you will ever have.

It doesn't matter whether you received your gift in a courtroom or a delivery room, the fact is, you are now a full-fledged member of a highly elite club. Members include teen mothers, single mothers, married mothers, adoptive mothers, stepmothers, stay-at-home mothers and working mothers. And while they come from various walks of life and various racial, social and economic backgrounds, they all share a common bond: They are mothers. No other event makes you so much an adult as becoming a mother: not education, establishing a career, buying a car, getting married or buying a house. And no other event changes you in such surprising and revealing ways as becoming a mother.

In order to maintain membership in the Motherhood Club, you must pay never-ending dues. They are tallied every time you kiss, hold, feed, burp, bathe, dress, undress, rock, shelter, protect and pray for your baby, and for yourself. I can attest to the fact that you will rely more and more on your religious faith as you settle into your most challenging and rewarding role. Sometimes, you will pray out loud; other times, you will mumble incoherently under your breath as you make your way through the first couple of weeks of mothering. I call that the "initiation period."

The initiation period is the time it takes to adjust to having a baby and to being a mother. It is one of the most physically, emotionally and psychologically challenging experiences you will ever have. It is a time when you will break down and cry, but you won't know why. It is a time when you will look in a mirror and hate everything about your body. And it is a time when you will exude the splendor of motherhood outside, but feel strong mixed emotions inside. That can be awfully confusing at times because society expects motherhood to be "the most wonderful time in your life." But the truth of the matter is we aren't very good about anticipating fear, panic and disenchantment. Those feelings aren't portrayed in the average media advertisements about motherhood.

The initiation period is also filled with intense change, much like the adjustment period after any other major life transition. For example, it is expected and perfectly understandable to have tears and doubts before your wedding, or to take time to feel like a couple with your new spouse. We expect to have to settle into a new job, or to take weeks to make a new house feel like home. And yet we expect to *automatically* feel like a mother. While some mothers settle into their new role in a matter of days, others take weeks or longer. The important thing is they adjust, and so will you.

The initiation period can be so overwhelming you will feel like you are losing your mind, but you're not. I know you are probably thinking, "That will never happen to me." Let me assure you, it will. All new mothers experience anxieties in one form or another. They are common and are inherent realities of being a mother. Therefore, there is no reason to fear being misunderstood, or feel ashamed. Joy, wonder, guilt, doubt and terror are all understandable because of the enormity of the change in your life and the importance of your new role. Honesty on this issue is very freeing. And knowing other new mothers have these feelings can help you feel not only less guilty but more connected with other mothers. That, of course, is good news.

The other good news is that members of the Motherhood Club will help you overcome the tremendous challenges you are facing. As you travel the road to motherhood you will run into emotional and physical roadblocks. Don't worry. The members of the Motherhood Club will help you navigate around them as you find your way. They have journeyed many miles down the path of motherhood. They know where the barriers are and they know the road is paved with three M's: miracles, magic and misery.

Through their strong, encouraging voices, the members will discuss the challenges they encountered while nestling into motherhood. They will share how they felt happy one minute and sad the next. They will share how they focused solely on their babies and neglected their mates. They will share how they smiled in the glow of motherhood and felt extremely happy most of the time. And they will share how they triumphed over their trials.

When you are stricken with basic anxieties, or what I call "Mother's Moody Blues," don't think for a second that you are the only one who has ever been hit with them. Because as much as you will want to believe that, you do not, I repeat, *do not* have exclusive rights to "Mother's Moody Blues." Members of the Motherhood Club will tell you that and a whole lot more.

Think back for just a second. Remember when you first found out you were pregnant? All attention focused directly on your baby, right? Your mate felt and kissed your stomach. Your doctor carefully calculated your baby's due date. Your mother was so thrilled about becoming a grandmother she shared the wonderful news with anyone who would listen. And your girlfriends, who are at your side no matter what, couldn't wait to give you a baby shower. They made sure the colors and theme were perfect, the games were fun, and the food and drink were delicious. But in the midst of all the excitement, no one bothered to tell you about the emotional ups and downs of mothering—not until now, that is. That is the mission of the Motherhood Club. Through the members' fiercely personal and inspiring stories you will learn some of the most common emotional, physical and psychological effects of mothering and how to deal with them.

Each mother's story is organized around myths and themes she found most influential during her adjustment to motherhood. While some chapters contain only one story, others may contain up to three. They are followed by expert clinical analysis and explanations about the changes the mothers went through and the strategies that helped ease the adjustments in their lives. You will also learn concrete tools for handling your new life and role. And you will understand why you are experiencing a flood of emotions during what is supposed to be the happiest time of your life. And it will be, once you get through the initiation period.

Just remember, you are in a new club now—the Motherhood Club. Life as you know it will never be the same. Everything you were accustomed to in your old world has changed tremendously. You now inhabit a new world that is filled with wonder and life-altering challenges. Want a good night's sleep? Forget about it. Feeling spontaneous? Plan for it. Feeling frisky? Not today or tomorrow.

And don't forget you have also changed. Your body has gone through a traumatic experience and a dramatic transformation from head to toe. Can't wear those cute little jeans anymore? Buy new ones. Milk flows like a river from your breasts? Buy extra nursing pads. Your mind is playing tricks on you? Beat it at its own game. Believe me, you will survive "Mother's Moody Blues."

And the members of the Motherhood Club will be with you every step of the way. They will hold your hand tightly as you make it through the initiation period. And when you reach the brighter side of mothering—and you will—you will be extremely proud and honored to be a member of the Motherhood Club. Congratulations!

I Am a Mother

From the moment you were conceived
to the moment I felt you move inside me
I knew I was a mother.

From the moment I held you in my arms
to the moment I knew I would always love you
I knew I was a mother.

From the moment I saw your beautiful face
to the moment I felt the warmth of your breath
I knew I was a mother.

From the moment I felt tremendous fear
to the moment it disappeared
I knew I was a mother.

From the moment I raised my first question
to the moment I knew it wouldn't be the last
I knew I was a mother.

From the moment I felt responsible for you
to the moment I prayed for guidance
I knew I was a mother.

From the moment I knew you would face barriers
to the moment I knew I would help you overcome them
I knew I was a mother.

From the moment I saw tears of sadness stain your face
to the moment I prayed there would be few
I knew I was a mother.

From the moment I saw your eyes filled with wonder
to the moment I prayed all your dreams would come true
I knew I was a mother.

From the moment I saw you take your first steps
to the moment I prayed your path would always be safe
I knew I was a mother.

From the moment I knew you would change the world
to the moment I knew I would always hold you in my heart
I knew I was a mother.

—Shirley Washington

One

A Mother's Life— "The Mothering Instinct" Myth

Mothering Instinct— Myth or Reality?

When you announced you were expecting, you were likely told some version of the myth of the "mothering instinct." ("Relax, you will know what to do!" "Don't worry, the minute you get your baby in your arms, you will do just fine!") The reality is mothering is not that simple. Sure, experience with infants is very helpful. You may have a natural ease with many parts of caring for your small arrival. You will know how to love that baby because you have learned to love. At the same time, you may be terrified about other parts of the job, such as how to detect a fever or give your baby a bath. The reality is you will bring many skills from other parts of your life to the job of parenting, and you will have many new skills to learn.

My name is Shirley Washington.
I am a television news anchor and reporter,
and the proud mother of a
beautiful little boy.

Baby's Name: _Curtis_

Date of Birth: _November 30, 1995_

Time of Birth: _5:30 A.M._

Weight: _6 pounds, 9.9 ounces_

Length: _20 ½ inches_

When my husband and I decided to have a baby we knew the time was right. We had been married nearly eight years, we were established in our respective careers and we had a burning desire to become parents. After making our momentous decision to start a family, I went to visit my obstetrician/gynecologist to share our hopes of having a baby. My doctor gave me a thorough examination, advised me to stop using contraceptives, and let nature take its course.

It didn't take long for me to conceive. About two months after I visited my doctor I discovered I was pregnant. It was as if my husband and I sipped juice from the same crystal flute, marking the beginning of my journey to motherhood. Even after my doctor confirmed my pregnancy, it was hard to believe that in nine months I was going to be a mother. I was thrilled. Overjoyed. And filled with anticipation. I fell in love with my baby instantly. And I couldn't wait to feel him growing inside of me—to experience the precious miracle of life. As my baby developed and kicked my stomach as if it were a soccer ball on an indoor field, I became more and more excited about becoming a mother.

> *I was afraid no one would understand if I said, "I'm very happy, I love my baby with all of my heart, but I'm nervous, scared and overwhelmed with mothering."*
>
> —SHIRLEY WASHINGTON

I will never forget the day my baby was born. It was a cool, crisp, fall morning. I got out of bed, took a shower, grabbed a bite to eat and drove to work as usual. Being a television news general assignment reporter, I covered a wide range of stories. On this particular Wednesday, November 29, 1995, I went to the Richard B. Russell Federal Courthouse in Atlanta, Georgia, to cover a police corruption hearing. While waiting for the proceedings to begin I sat in the courtroom with a few of my colleagues laughing and talking about a number of events, including the day's news.

Looking around the room, I noticed C. B. Hackworth, a producer from a competing television station, walking through the imposing courtroom doors. I often teased C. B. because he looked like Neil Patrick Harris, the actor who played a teenage doctor on the hit television show *Doogie Howser, M.D.,* and this day was no exception. My lips curled into a smile as I exclaimed, "Thank goodness, there's Doogie Howser. He can deliver my baby if I go into labor."

Of course, I was only kidding. However, a few minutes later—much to my surprise—my water broke! In federal court! I couldn't believe it! I was in labor! My baby, the baby I loved and longed to hold was about to be born. I remember feeling a myriad of emotions as I sat on a bench in the front row of the courtroom. But mainly I was in shock and couldn't believe I was in labor in federal court of all places. I was excited, anxious and deeply embarrassed. There I was in the midst of prominent attorneys, bailiffs and members of the media with water gushing down my legs. Yes, I was in labor all right! This was far from the way I had imagined things would be, but it was my reality.

I leaned over to Kevin Maggoire, my photographer, and whispered in his ear as calmly and as nonchalantly as possible, "My water just broke." Kevin's eyes nearly popped out of their sockets. Stunned, he stared at me as if I was a visitor from another planet. Kevin was probably thinking, *This isn't supposed to happen on my watch.* During my pregnancy some of the news photographers I worked with on a regular basis told me repeatedly that they were not going to shoot stories for me during the last month of my pregnancy: They didn't want to have to rush me to the hospital.

Some of the photographers were kidding and others, well, they were serious. I didn't blame them. They had seen Hollywood's dramatic version of irate women giving birth in delivery rooms. They had seen television sitcoms that tried to make light of screaming women in delivery rooms. And some of them had been in delivery rooms with their own wives. So they were familiar with the ups and downs of labor. My colleagues made it crystal clear they wanted to avoid the "downs."

After fumbling with my briefcase and spilling nearly all of its contents onto the courtroom floor, Kevin glared at me with alarming eyes. "You don't look like your water broke," he said in a nervous, matter-of-fact tone. For a split second, and only a second, I remember thinking, *What does an expectant mother whose water broke look like?* Instead of responding, I stood up from the bench, grabbed my coat, and retrieved my wallet and other items that had escaped from my briefcase. Kevin stared at the river that streamed down the wooden bench behind me and exclaimed, "Oh my God, your water did break," in a loud panicky voice that captured everyone's attention—including Patrick Crosby, public affairs officer for the United States Department of Justice and U.S. Attorney's Office. Patrick ran to get paper towels and soaked up the water with a swift speed that would have impressed Olympic gold medalist Michael Johnson.

Being the gentleman that he is, Kevin rushed me to the hospital in his television news vehicle. But not before we had a heated debate about whether I should go home first. "I can't deliver my baby like this. I want to take a shower!" I yelled. My argument for cleanliness paled in the face of Kevin's strong reasoning. After pointing out I risked getting caught in rush hour traffic and delivering my baby on the side of the highway, I quickly climbed into the news vehicle and we drove straight to the hospital.

Deeply concerned about my well-being and that of my unborn baby, Kevin was careful not to hit any bumps along the way. Fear, however, tried more than once to persuade him to exceed the speed limit. At my insistence Kevin obeyed the law after I assured him I was fine and my baby was fine. We arrived at Northside Hospital safely and without incident. And Kevin stayed with me for nearly an hour until my husband arrived. What a guy!

I was in intense labor for about eleven and a half hours when my doctor told me and my husband that I had to have an emergency C-section. My baby was in distress. He was pushing, trying to enter the world, but I had not dilated enough. The mere thought of having surgery made my heart pound louder and faster than normal. It was beating so fast and so loud I felt like someone was standing on either side of me, holding snare drums next to each of my ears and pounding like crazy.

For the first time during labor I was afraid of the unknown. It was the kind of fear I had never felt before. Knowing my baby was trying to make an entrance into the world, but couldn't, was too much to bear. Besides pain, I didn't think there was anything to worry about during childbirth. *Why should there be?* I thought. *Women have babies every day and most of them don't suffer any complications.*

About an hour later my beautiful baby boy was born. Tears rolled down my radiant face when I heard his high-pitched voice. And when I held my baby in my arms for the first time it felt like everything around me was suddenly still and quiet, except for my little angel. I had never been so happy or thankful for the absolute best gift I had ever received—my son. I held my baby for what seemed like hours, rubbing his head, kissing his cheeks and looking at his little body in complete awe. And then I prayed, giving thanks for my wonderful blessing. I promised the Lord and my son that I would be the best mother I could possibly be.

Four days later, my husband and I took our son home. As we drove toward our house I couldn't wait to take our baby to the nursery. I could see it vividly in my mind's eye. My husband and I had painted the room sky blue and adorned the walls with thick, white, puffy clouds and angels. We created "A Baby from Heaven" theme, because we believe babies come from heaven—we also hadn't learned the gender of our baby before he was born. We figured a heavenly design was appropriate for a boy or girl.

As the pictures continued to flash in my mind, I could see the white crib, white changing table and white rocking chair strategically placed in the nursery. Suddenly, it occurred to me that I didn't know the first thing about caring for a baby— my baby. Oh sure, I had all of the necessary supplies: diapers, bottles, blankets, bassinet and a baby bed, but I didn't have the wisdom, knowledge or know-how to care for my baby. Question after question swirled in my head: *What do I do when my baby cries? Gets a fever? Won't latch on?* I had absolutely no idea. Without warning, I felt intense fear. Not the kind I experienced during delivery, but fear nonetheless.

As we pulled into the driveway, I looked at my adorable son. He was sound asleep in his infant car seat—without a care in the world. Covered in a soft, blue, wool blanket, my son squirmed as if he was going to awake. Nervous, my hands trembled as I unbuckled the straps and removed him from the car seat. I held my baby as tightly as I could and thought about the road ahead as we entered the house.

Dragging my right leg, I made it to the nursery with my baby without incident. I was concerned he would awake because of my interesting-sounding gait and uneven steps. The muscles in my lower back and leg were so sore after delivery

I couldn't bend my leg. But it was nothing six weeks of physical therapy couldn't cure, and quite frankly, it wasn't anything I was overly concerned about. At that point, all of my attention was focused squarely on my son.

In the following days, I had more energy than the Energizer Bunny. If my baby even *looked* like he wanted to cry, I was there instantly—feeding, rocking or changing him. However, I became nervous when I gave my baby a bath. I was afraid I would hurt his tender, fragile body, or drop him when he was slippery and wet. Even though my mother and mother-in-law came to visit on separate occasions to help me care for my son, I was afraid to ask them or friends basic questions about mothering. I thought they would think less of me because I didn't know the answers—answers I thought came naturally the moment I joined the Motherhood Club.

One day, my baby was screaming at the top of his lungs and I had absolutely no idea why he was crying. He wasn't hungry, he wasn't wet and he wasn't sleepy. But I couldn't comfort him to save my life. Realizing I was clueless, my mother took my son, wrapped him in a warm blanket and rocked him in my favorite chair. And like magic he stopped crying within seconds. I just stood in the doorway mesmerized as my mother worked her magic. I felt miserable and guilty because I didn't know what to do. And I was too ashamed to say anything or ask for help.

A few weeks later, my husband was giving our baby a bath and he couldn't figure out how to clean our son's nose. He tried a bulb syringe, but it wasn't effective. By this time my mom had gone home. My husband called his mother long distance to ask her what to do. I was so embarrassed and upset my temperature soared near boiling. Obviously, my husband did the right thing. However, at the time, the simple act of calling someone for help made me feel inadequate as a mother. And served as an absolute admission that I didn't know basic baby care. "She must think I am the worst mother in the world because I don't know how to clean our baby's nose," I said. But I was wrong. My mother-in-law merely suggested what to do and offered to answer any questions anytime.

I couldn't believe it. I was an educated career woman—an award-winning television news anchor/reporter—who was afraid to ask questions. I made a living interviewing people— everyone from high-profile politicians to everyday, ordinary people. But yet, I was afraid to query my family and friends about how to care for my sweet, defenseless baby.

I felt badly for not knowing the basics, for not asking questions and for having anxieties when I performed simple tasks like bathing my son. I was frustrated and confused because when I was pregnant all I heard was how wonderful and rewarding mothering is, and it is. However, no one told me I would be riding an emotional roller coaster after my baby was born, that I would feel so many emotions that changed constantly, like colors on a signal light.

I didn't dare tell anyone about the feelings that enveloped me. I was afraid no one would understand if I said, "I'm very happy, I love my baby with all of my heart, but I'm nervous, scared and overwhelmed with mothering." So I held my tongue and hid behind an invisible wall of frustration. I also became very protective of my son. I wouldn't leave him with anyone because I didn't think anyone could care for him better than I could, even though I didn't have a clue about how to do that.

One night, my baby had a fever. I didn't know how to get his temperature back to normal. Panic stricken, I called an emergency hotline number listed on one of the brochures I received from the hospital. I told a nurse on the end of the line my newborn baby had a fever, was crying uncontrollably and was very irritable. I asked if I could bring him to the emergency room to be examined by a doctor. The nurse asked me several questions, gave me medical advice and suggested I wait until morning to make an appointment with my son's pediatrician.

A couple of hours later, my baby was still burning with fever, and screaming at the top of his lungs. Needless to say I was scared. I called the nurse again and asked if I could bring him in to be checked by a doctor. The nurse asked more questions and again suggested I wait until the next day to make an appointment with my baby's doctor. That's when I lost what little control I had. I started crying and yelling into the phone, "I am a new mother, my baby has a fever, he won't stop crying and I'm scared. At what point do you deem it necessary to have him examined by a doctor? When he's dead?" Silence fell on the line. A couple of seconds later, the nurse advised me to bring my baby to the emergency room right away.

I was deeply embarrassed by my rude behavior and

completely shocked by my stern, panic-stricken voice—a voice I didn't recognize. At that point, however, I didn't care about being prim and proper or identifying my voice. I was only concerned about getting help for my baby. My desire to do so was driven by something innate that swelled within me. At the emergency room, after giving my baby a thorough examination, the doctor diagnosed my son with an ear infection, wrote a prescription and told me he was going to be fine.

That night was a turning point for me as a new mother because I realized the importance of asking questions, asking for help and being persistent. And I learned not to be so hard on myself for not knowing basic baby care. How could I have known? I had never been a mother before. And I had not spent a lot of time around infants.

Because of my inexperience I found the first couple of weeks of motherhood stressful and overwhelming. I was tired and frustrated. Sometimes I found myself throwing my hands into the air and sighing deeply as I wondered if I was ever going to learn the skills needed to care for my baby. I constantly prayed for strength, guidance and an attitude adjustment. I was in desperate need of a new attitude because while I had developed the courage to ask questions, I was not confident as a mother and I felt inadequate.

When my joy started sinking I searched shelves at local bookstores and libraries looking for books about first-time mothers and the challenges they face as they settle into motherhood. Unfortunately, I didn't find any. So I began to talk with other mothers about their trials and triumphs during their first few weeks of mothering. I found comfort in their personal stories: They were mothers who had been in the grip of fear; mothers who had cried a river of tears (but couldn't explain why); mothers who had experienced sheer bliss that came and went like the wind.

They assured me it was okay to feel that mothering was not what I had dreamed it would be in the beginning—because it rarely lives up to our fantasies. But it does get better and better with each passing day. They also assured me that I was, in fact, "okay" and a "good mother." That validation made me feel revitalized and my confidence catapulted to a higher level that felt both unfamiliar and somehow comfortable.

As I embraced my new attitude, I was forced to closely examine my situation and take control. It became clear to me that I had to accept the fact that I was a new mother who possessed little to no mothering skills. But I believed that time would help me learn, hone and master those skills if I worked at them. Once I accepted that, I was able to move forward.

Along the way I realized I had to take "mommy moments" and get in touch with my spirit—I mean really sit down and get in tune with *me*. I figured if I didn't help myself climb out of the rut I had fallen into, I was not going to be capable of helping anyone else—not my baby, husband, family, friends— or myself. Armed with new confidence, I decided to spend quality time alone with me. I took a few minutes a day to concentrate on feeling good about me as a mother. Sometimes, after I put my baby down for a nap, I would prepare a peaches-and-cream bubble bath, slip into the warm soothing water, relax and think positive thoughts about my mothering skills.

Or I would sleep, read or listen to my favorite music. In fact, legendary R&B singer Patti LaBelle's hit tune "New Attitude" became my theme song. "Mommy moments" helped me relax so that I could focus on the progress I was making instead of my lack of mothering skills. Every time I completed a task without incident I gave myself a "that-a-girl" and an "A." For instance, if I gave my baby a bath and didn't worry about dropping him, or if I failed to panic because my baby was crying (and I didn't have the slightest idea why), but remained calm and solved the problem, I gave myself a pat on the back.

It wasn't long before I learned to stare fear in the face and stand strong. I also learned to laugh at myself for being intimidated by that four-letter word. With fear far behind me, I started a new ritual. I repeated a simple affirmation to myself several times a day: *I can do this.* Before I reached that point, however, it was imperative for me to push my fears aside. I had to start believing I was a good mother and could do an excellent job caring for my baby.

Once I cleansed my mind and spirit of everything negative, learned to trust myself and made it a daily ritual to take "mommy moments," I was able to properly care for my baby without as much fear or worry. I soon realized that for every detour and curve I discovered while traveling the path of motherhood, there are straightaways that lead to unwavering confidence and happiness. I also learned new mothers reach that destination at different times, but the important thing is that they do get there. You will, too. That's why I decided to write *The Motherhood Club:* to let you know you are not alone. You will develop the confidence and skills you need to care for your baby. You will overcome the challenges that go along with mothering. You will emerge triumphantly and enjoy the splendor of motherhood the way it was meant to be!

Shirley's Savvy Strategies

- Trust yourself. Build your trust by listing each of your daily successes as evidence of your growing competence.
- Identify skills you have in other parts of your life. Look for ways those skills apply to parenting.
- Talk positively to yourself: "You can do it," or "Good job!"
- Take time for yourself each day. Five minutes a couple times a day is helpful in refueling.
- Connect with other women, for reassurance and for sharing knowledge.

The "Mothering Instinct" Myth

Myths about new motherhood are powerful yet subtle. Women hear them every day, and they seep into our brains, often without our awareness. We are all susceptible, no matter how rational or educated we may seem on the surface. Shirley's story illustrates one of the major myths, the myth of the "mothering instinct." New mothers are told: "Relax, you will know what to do the minute you get your baby in your arms" or "Being a mother comes naturally." If you really have no experience with babies, it is absolutely terrifying to think you should know what to do when you don't have a clue!

Sometimes we play into the myth. We may believe all human beings (not just women) have some level of instinct about what to do with a baby. Or maybe we believe that since we were parented well, we can rely on what we have learned by observation or personal experience. And we may think to ourselves: *I am a competent person in many ways. I have handled a boardroom full of executives (or cantankerous politicians, or a room full of ten-year-olds); surely, I can handle one baby.* We expect our competence in one area to carry over to handling a new baby as well. Let's lay this out for what it is: a myth—and a dangerous one at that. Dangerous because it isolates us, keeps us from admitting that we don't know it all or don't feel instantly like a perfect mother.

There is no other job on earth for which we are less prepared by our society than the job of being a mother (or father). Any other new job you had of this level of importance came with a bit more training than the twenty-minute class on diapering and bathing offered in the average hospital. You would not be handed the keys to a bulldozer or an eighteen-wheeler and told, "Trust your instincts—you will know what to do." Good solid training and a definitive procedural manual would be essential. And just *one* manual, with the right way clearly laid out—not forty or fifty to choose from at your nearest bookstore. Of course you are confused by mothering! Who wouldn't be?

Resisting the Myth

Realizing you have had minimal training at parenting may not be enough to bring your expectations of yourself in line with the reality. You may, like most new parents, succumb to this myth even though you lack experience. Even though messages in our culture lead you, and others, to think that you should be able to do this job automatically, banish those false expectations from your brain. Follow the steps outlined here to begin to battle these faulty ideas:

- Be easier on yourself. It is hard to know what to do when you have never done this job. You would not expect to walk into any other job and just "know" what to do. Remind yourself that you will get better with time.
- You need training, information and input. Ask questions, observe other mothers or take a class.

- Even with input, you also need practice. Realize that you have to work at anything you want to do well—including being a parent.

When you start a new job, you usually get a probationary or training period before your employer truly expects you to be able to do the job *well*. Allow yourself an adjustment period for your new parenting job as well.

The Initiation Period

Shirley accurately identifies the "Initiation Period." The idea of an adjustment or initiation period is helpful in moving your thinking away from the idea that being a mother is instantaneous. The moment you give birth you do become a mother—literally. But don't allow yourself to believe that birth is the end of the "becoming" part. Becoming a mother in function and feeling is a process, not an either/or proposition. It is an ongoing journey, a path you travel down, making mistakes, hesitating and being confused, developing confidence over time, until you *truly* feel and act like a mother. Becoming a mother is not a black-and-white transition. You can't be childless and self-focused one day, than instantly "become a mother"—with all the inner wisdom you will ever need—the next day. You have to take it bit by bit, learning along the way about yourself and your baby's ever-developing needs and personality.

Work to trust yourself, as Shirley did, and you will find your way. Look at the many skills you have that apply to being a mother. You may be patient, a good problem-solver, an able learner, willing to ask for help. Write down those skills, use them, take deep breaths, persist, work together with your partner. Shirley's strategies of talking positively to herself and taking time to rest, relax and refuel are time-tested tools to make the process easier. Above all, remember that you do not have to know it all. You are not born with this knowledge. Allow yourself to seek out experts—other mothers who can share their knowledge with you. Shirley found this connection to other mothers very powerful.

Remind yourself that you are not deficient if mothering does not feel natural. You are simply a new mother, who will find a style that works for you, after some ups and downs and trial and error. Babies are not as fragile as they appear, and there is not a woman out there who has not stumbled a bit along the way to becoming a "good enough" mother!

Two

Baby Bliss—
Living the Myth

Blissful Motherhood: Myth or Reality?

Television, films, advertisements in magazines, even classic Old World art masterpieces show scenes of glowing mothers with happy, beautiful, calm babies. Accurate portrayals are rare. When was the last time you saw a magazine ad with a crying, wrinkled baby and a cranky mom in a tattered bathrobe, dark circles under her eyes, and mussed hair on her head? Both pictures can, and do, happen. Both sides of life with a new baby are real. The reality is that the glowing, happy times can balance out with dark, tired times—especially after a couple of weeks.

My name is Donna Thomson. I am a business owner and the proud mother of a beautiful little boy.

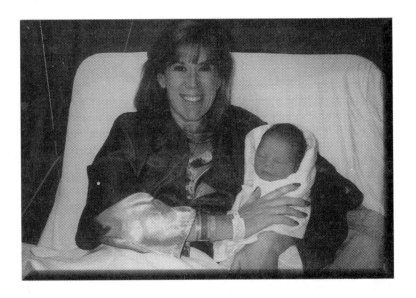

Baby's Name: *Noah*

Date of Birth: *December 9, 1996*

Time of Birth: *9:45 A.M.*

Weight: *7 pounds, 13 ounces*

Length: *21 inches*

When I found out I was pregnant, joy swelled inside of me like a surge of electricity. Smiling to myself, I suddenly felt as if I was glowing from the inside out. Carrying my baby and feeling him growing inside me surpassed all my expectations. It was an extraordinary experience that was thrilling and exciting from beginning to end.

I was overcome with great emotion when my beautiful baby boy was born. It was magnified a million times when my anesthesiologist serenaded my son. Clearing his throat, the doctor raised his tenor voice in song. All eyes focused on the doctor, dressed in

> *I was so elated I found myself crying tears of joy almost every time I looked at my baby.*
>
> —DONNA THOMSON

scrubs, as he sang "Happy Birthday" to my newborn baby. His voice quickly filled my heart (as well as the delivery room!). As each note floated slowly through the air, my emotions soared higher and higher. I was mesmerized.

It was the most wonderful rendition of "Happy Birthday" I had ever heard. Of course, I had heard the song a hundred times before. And I had sung it myself on occasions. But on that day, at that moment, it felt as if I was hearing it for the very first time: "Happy *Birth*day." The day my little Noah was born.

It was a fiercely special moment that was only enhanced by the sound of my baby's voice chiming in with a tune of his own. If I had to give that tune a name, I would have called it the "Baby Duck" song. That's what Noah sounded like when he was born—a sweet little baby duck. The instant I heard his shrill voice, cracking and quacking, I turned to my sister and my best friend and asked, "What's that duck doing in here?" They laughed and answered, "That's not a duck. That's your baby."

My baby. The baby I had waited so long to meet was finally here. When my doctor placed Noah on my chest I couldn't see him at first. He was too close. He was resting directly under my chin. I wrapped my arms around Noah gently and pulled him back. The instant I saw his precious face tears fell from my eyes. I was so happy. I felt like I had waited an eternity to meet my baby. What a moment!

I was so pleased to have Noah because I didn't think I would ever have children. I was thirty-eight years old. I wasn't married. And children were not a part of my plans. As I looked at Noah in complete awe a wave of jubilation fell over me. I was grateful to have such a wonderful little person to care for. And, eventually, care for me. That, in and of itself, made a tremendous impact on me. I was so happy, I found myself crying tears of joy almost every time I looked at Noah.

I must admit I was pleasantly surprised by my feelings. Before Noah was born I was not a very emotional person, not by any stretch of the imagination. After being single for so long, I had become slightly hardened around the edges, and I had a strong sense of self. My attitude was: This is who I am. . . . This is how I'm going to run things. . . . This is what I stand for.

When Noah came into my life I began to soften. I felt my emotions more intensely, and I began to realize I was no longer the center of my world. I transitioned into my new role with surprisingly graceful ease. I was in baby heaven—especially when I brought Noah home from the hospital. I couldn't get enough of him. I was so protective of and very careful with him. I remember being concerned initially about dropping him, and I hesitated to walk around the house with him in my arms, because I thought I would run into a door and he would fall to the floor. I know that sounds absurd, but when you walk around by yourself, you don't pay much attention to the process; you just get up and go. When you're walking and holding a baby, however, you think twice about it—you're carrying precious cargo.

Thank goodness I got over that "dropping" phase within days and went back to enjoying my baby. I was blissfully happy and so taken with Noah. There were times I would stand by the side of his crib for what seemed like hours and watch him sleep. Joyous tears streamed down my face, and through those tears I could see so clearly: Noah was a reflection of me, and I was responsible for him.

I loved taking care of Noah—even when I was dead tired or in pain from my C-section. I couldn't wait to coddle and lavish him with never-ending love. It didn't matter if it was day or night, if Noah so much as whimpered because he was hungry or needed changing, I ran to him without hesitating. I just thought, *My baby needs me.* I loved that. I never knew I possessed such unselfish, caring and giving characteristics until my baby forced them to surface.

Over the years, before my son was born, I had grown accustomed to thinking only about *me* and caring only for *me*. I didn't have time for anyone else, let alone a baby. But Noah changed all of that. It was as if someone slapped my face and said in a loud booming voice that rattled the rafters, "It's no longer about you!" Instead of being afraid, I accepted that reality, and I absorbed the message that rang out loud and clear.

Being a mother stirred so many wonderful emotions within me. I found myself making new discoveries about my feelings almost every day. Whenever I watched the news on television and there was a report about a missing child I cried. Or if there was a report about a child reuniting with his family I cried. And if Noah did something—anything, no matter how small—I really went over the edge. When Noah cut teeth I was emotional. The first time Noah reached out to me I was emotional. When Noah hugged me I was emotional.

Getting in touch with my emotional side proved to be an eye-opening experience in more ways than one. It was during that time that I realized not only the wonderful joy a baby can bring, but how precious and significant life is. All of a sudden, my family and friends became more important to me. There were times when I found myself calling my sister or girlfriend to share Noah's accomplishments without thinking twice about it. I was so proud of him. I wanted to let the world know everything about him.

I also wanted my family and friends to share our joy and be a part of Noah's life. Because of *his* life, I learned to appreciate, love and respect other lives more—a lot more than I ever had in the past. That also made my eyes brim with tears. Sometimes, when my emotions got the best of me and I found myself crying, I would hold Noah in my arms and give thanks for him. Or I would let go, have a really hard cry and get over it.

Realizing how blessed I am to have Noah helps me cope with so many moments in my new life. No matter where I am or how I'm feeling, my mind takes me back to Noah's birthday—the day he made his grand entrance into the world. I love reliving that special moment because in a sense, that was also the day I was reborn.

Donna's Savvy Strategies

- Embrace your feelings—positive and negative.
- Acknowledge that your feelings are real, deserve to be felt and can help you be a better mother.
- Connect with friends and family—you are not embarking on motherhood alone.

Baby Bliss—"Living" the Myth

Donna's story illustrates a universal truth—having a baby is life-altering. You will never be the same person after motherhood that you were when you were childless. Becoming a mother often surprises us. We discover parts of ourselves that we have not had the opportunity to see in previous roles in our lives. Often, being a mother is the first time a woman is called upon to give so unselfishly, to be relied upon so totally.

The new mother has to switch focus from self to other. How gratifying to find, as Donna did, that we do have this ability within us. Jane Weaver, an academic psychologist at University College, London, and her postgraduate student Jane Ussher, interviewed thirteen first-time mothers about how motherhood had changed their lives. They found that this ability to change priorities from self to child was one of the biggest surprises about becoming a parent.

While pregnant, these women admitted that being a parent would require self-sacrifice. But not having been parents before, that was just a concept. They did not have a sense of how that felt in real life. When their babies were born, their ability to sacrifice for the child astounded them, just as it did Donna. They did not know they had it in them. Just as surprising for the women in this study was the sense of overwhelming love they felt for their new babies. Even though they may have loved and felt loved in previous relationships, they were awed by the power of the love they felt for their children.

Donna's experience shows us that, while still stereotypes, "the perfect mother" and "love at first sight" syndromes do exist. What makes ideals like these into stereotypes or myths is the frequency with which they occur. Does every new mother love the job or feel overwhelming love for her baby at first glance? Certainly, these myths can be reality. Many women feel a perfect fit with motherhood and bask in the glow of caring for a small baby. This is how it was for Donna. She was living the myth. But the fact that everybody does not experience new motherhood in this way is why we challenge these ideals as myths or inaccurate stereotypes.

Reassure yourself that you are a good person and a good enough parent, even if your introduction to being a mom does not match the ideal picture. But know, too, that if your experience does fit this myth, you are one of the lucky ones, because your expectations match your reality.

A Hidden Myth

One myth underlying the adjustment to motherhood is the idea that "I can keep my life unchanged." Many women are disappointed after the birth of a baby because the disruption to their lives is *so* drastic. Certainly you may have thought your life would change, but you had no idea about the degree. Most women do not voice this myth, hence it is hidden. They only think it, never admitting out loud, "My life will not change." Since this myth is not spoken, it is harder to recognize and combat. It may make you feel badly without knowing why.

Recognize that:

- You are not deficient.
- You are not alone in feeling your life has changed.
- It is pretty impossible to keep your life the same as it was before you became a mother.
- Embrace the change, as Donna did, and look at the ways in which you are growing as a person while your baby grows.

Donna's life before parenthood had been focused on other needs—surviving, defining herself, achieving career success. Through Noah, she increased her awareness of the value of connecting to others. She opened herself to the joy in giving, in loving others. Then these feelings generalized from baby Noah to others whom she loved, such as friends and family. As we grow into adults, we first must focus to define ourselves: *Who am I? What do I stand for? What can I contribute?* Donna was used to centering all her energy on these questions, until Noah came into her life. Then she quickly saw the value of nurturing another life, which in many developmental theories is a major task of adulthood.

Navigating Relationship Changes

Donna's story illustrates the inevitable changes in our relationships to others that come with being a parent. Donna became more connected to her friends and family, sharing the joy she felt at Noah's every milestone. This is one way relationships can change when a woman becomes a parent: She feels connected more to other mothers; she is more in touch with her emotional side and shares those feelings with her support system.

Equally common changes in relationships include distance or conflict after the birth of a baby. The new mother may be the only one of her friends with a child, and her friends or colleagues may not share her enthusiasm for every cute development in her baby. Friends may have a different focus in their lives and tire of all the baby talk. The new mother may lose interest in previously shared activities—for instance, she couldn't care less about office gossip now that she is out of that setting. Friends may come around less, and the new mom finds herself with limited time to socialize. This loss weighs heavily on many new mothers. She misses her old friends and feels isolated until she can connect with new friends who may be parents themselves.

Understanding Changing Hormones

To accomplish as much as she had to this point in her life, Donna may have grown into the habit of conquering her emotions. Staying focused on rational thought and facts may have been necessary for her to accomplish her goals and define herself. Emotions may have been too distracting to these ends, so she learned to push them aside. Then, when she was exposed to the vulnerability that a baby naturally shows, she was able to allow her own vulnerability to surface.

The changing hormones of pregnancy and the immediate postpartum period may have had a role as well in bringing her emotions to the surface. These hormones make no bigger shift in a woman's lifetime than in the several days around the birth of a baby, going from all-time highs to equally all-time lows. Changes in progesterone, prolactin and estrogen, as well as many lesser-known female hormones, often have a direct effect on a woman's mood and feelings.

The exact way in which these hormones influence our moods is still not completely known. Recent evidence from the National Institute of Mental Health indicates that estrogen and progesterone have a direct physiologic effect on the brain. These hormones also affect the brain, to a lesser degree, by helping in the regulation of serotonin, dopamine and norepinephrine—all of which are brain hormones related to sleep, anxiety and mood.

For many women, the changes in these female and brain hormones result in negative feelings: 50 to 80 percent of new mothers get postpartum blues in the days or first few weeks after a baby is born. The blues are relatively mild mood swings, irritability, worries and tearfulness that are directly related to falling hormone levels. However, Donna was again one of the lucky ones: She had the "postpartum pinks" instead—all rosy happiness!

The only downside to the hormonal changes Donna experienced was the intense worry about hurting Noah, dropping him or running into a doorway. Worries like these, which seem less than rational, may be related to the rise in oxytocin in the new mother. Oxytocin has a role in starting labor contractions and in breastfeeding. While new moms have plenty of natural oxytocin, the synthetic form (Pitocin) is often used to speed up contractions during labor. Scientists know that oxytocin is also related to the mothering instinct.

When lab rats are given oxytocin, they begin to "mother" the baby lab rats, protecting and grooming them. So oxytocin may be the chemical that helps a new mother perceive dangers in her baby's world, and leads her to protect her baby. As with Donna, these dangers are often imagined rather than real. Hormonal changes eventually even out, and the new mother can then let go of the worries of those initial days.

Three

Baby Balance— The Good Mother Myth

Being a "Good Mother"— Myth or Reality?

Most women have preconceived ideas about the ways in which they want to be a "good mother." Of course you want to be one. No one would choose to be a "bad mother." Still, when we begin to list the ways in which we will be good mothers, myths can strongly influence us: "I will never yell at my kids" or "I will always be patient and loving." Watch out for those absolute qualifiers. It is nearly impossible to be *always* or *never* anything!

My name is Sarah Thomas.
I am a teacher, bandleader and proud mother
of beautiful twin girls.

Baby's Name: _Rachel_   Baby's Name: _Rebekah_

Date of Birth: _May 18, 2000_   Date of Birth: _May 18, 2000_

Time of Birth: _2:54 A.M._   Time of Birth: _2:55 A.M._

Weight: _3 pounds, 7 ounces_   Weight: _3 pounds, 7 ounces_

Length: _15 inches_   Length: _14 inches_

My husband and I walked around in a daze after a sonogram revealed I was carrying twins. While we were thrilled about the prospect of becoming parents we were stunningly surprised by the news. My husband kept repeating, "Two babies, two babies," under his breath as if in a deep trance. I was simply speechless. That was also shocking because I am rarely at a loss for words. When I was finally able to speak, I couldn't believe my ears when I heard myself telling people I was expecting twins. It sounded funny. Odd. Surreal.

I had suffered a miscarriage a few days before I learned I was pregnant with twins. All the emotions a mother feels after being told she has lost her precious baby embraced me. My doctor figured I must have been carrying triplets and lost one of the babies. It seemed weird to go from hearing "You lost a baby," to hearing "You're pregnant with two babies."

> *There were also times when I felt guilty about whether I was showing favoritism toward one baby over the other.*
>
> —SARAH THOMAS

My dad wasn't surprised at all. He expected it. Because his father was a twin, my dad predicted my sister or I was going to give birth to twins. In fact, when I told him I was pregnant the first time, he looked me straight in the eyes and said, "It's going to be you." Of course, I insisted he was wrong. However, it turns out Dad was right. My baby girls were born a minute a part, via C-section—eight weeks early.

When I first heard my daughters crying, their voices sounded like music to my ears. I asked my husband to check them right away. "You've got to go count their fingers and toes," I said. My husband's feet must have been bolted to the floor because he didn't budge. "Richard, honey, you've got to check on the babies," I pleaded. Looking at me with defiant eyes, he replied hesitantly, "Honey, I can't. They haven't sewn you up yet." The doctors were still working on me, after my C-section, and my husband was squeamish about seeing what they were doing.

As far as I was concerned, that was not a good excuse. "Put your hand up beside your face and go look at them," I demanded. Walking slowly, Richard went to check on our babies. When he returned his voice was filled with emotion. "They're so pretty. They're so pretty. And so tiny," was all he managed to say. *But what about their fingers and toes?* I wondered. A nurse wrapped my babies up in soft blankets and placed them gently in my welcoming arms. I was awestruck. Like my husband, I was amazed by how beautiful and small our babies were.

Rebekah and Rachel tipped the scales at exactly three pounds, seven ounces each. Because they were born two months early, I was concerned about whether they would encounter complications. The fact that they did not have to be rushed to a ventilator and that they were breathing on their own was very comforting. When I checked my babies and saw they had all their fingers and toes my eyes glistened with tears.

After three and a half weeks, Rachel and Rebekah had gained enough weight to go home. That wonderful news came one morning when my husband and I went to the hospital to feed them. We had been visiting our babies four times a day—feeding them, rocking them, holding them and lavishing them with love ever since I was released from the hospital three days after they were born. While I knew my husband and I were going to take our babies home, I was not prepared to take them that day. I didn't know what to do or how to care for them.

The wonderful nurses at the hospital did their best to make the transition from the facility to home as easy as possible. One of them took our babies into a small room as we followed closely behind. Sounding a lot like a college professor, the nurse gave my husband and me a crash course in how to care for our twins. When class was over she turned and walked out of the room. We were on our own. Thank goodness a nurse came to check on us every four hours. That was comforting because the nurses were right there to answer our questions.

Richard and I took our babies home the following day. I was excited and nervous because we were making the journey alone: Richard, the twins and me. No nurses. No doctors.

At home, the biggest challenge was getting the girls to sleep. Their internal clocks were off—way off. Rebekah and Rachel slept all day and were up all night. Richard and I were beyond exhaustion. I spent so many nights lying at the foot of our bed, leaning over the cradle, crying my eyes out and thinking, *I am a bad mother because I can't get my babies to sleep.* At the same time, my husband was rocking the cradle asking, "What are we doing wrong? Why won't they sleep?"

Some mornings my mother would call and ask whether the babies had slept through the night and instead of answering I would break down sobbing. She kept telling me I had to sleep when the girls slept, but that was so hard to do. There was so much to be done around the house: laundry, cooking and cleaning. I was so exhausted I had to surrender and let some of the chores go unattended.

My husband and I finally decided to take my mother's advice and start sleeping when the twins slept—even if it wasn't our bedtime. I was amazed what four hours of uninterrupted sleep with no babies crying did for my body. I was refreshed, but desperate to find a better solution for our situation. After reading several books that contained conflicting information about how to put infants to sleep, Richard and I figured out what worked best for us, then threw the books out the window. We started setting a bedtime, nap time and wake-up schedule for the girls instead of letting them decide when they would sleep and get up. Luckily, after trial and error, we finally managed to get the twins on a sleeping schedule within two months.

Mothering was starting to go well until I had a small setback. I began to wonder whether I was capable of loving both of my babies equally. That thought stayed at the forefront of my mind and made me feel guilty if I did something for one of my twins and not the other. For example, if I held Rebekah and not Rachel I felt guilty, or if I held Rachel longer than I held Rebekah, I felt guilty. And if I couldn't hold both babies at the same time, I wanted my husband to hold one of them so neither would think I loved the other more.

Try as I might, there was no escaping the guilt. There were also times when I felt guilty about whether I was showing favoritism toward one baby over the other. I knew I wasn't, but I felt as if I was. If I played with a musical toy with Rachel, I had to play with the same musical toy with Rebekah—and for the same amount of time. After a while I realized that that kind of absolute equality wasn't possible or practical.

Once I accepted the fact that I could not divide my love or time equally between my babies it was easier for me to care for them. I nursed the girls for eight weeks. I wanted to do it longer. However, breastfeeding two little ones at the same time proved to be more stressful than I anticipated. I labored over my decision to switch from breastfeeding to bottle-feeding. It was difficult because I felt like I was being a horrible mother if I didn't nurse my girls.

In the end, giving my babies formula turned out to be better for all of us. My daughters were getting fuller and were sleeping longer at night. On the other hand, I was still getting a workout with around-the-clock feedings, diaper changes and baths. During a typical day, I fed Rebekah and Rachel every three or four hours about six times a day. Each baby drank four or five ounces of formula per feeding. They went through a fourteen-and-a-half-ounce can in no time!

Diapering the girls also seemed to be a never-ending task. I changed Rebekah and Rachel ten to twenty times a day. It seemed like every time I got a clean diaper on them they had to be changed again. Or, in the middle of diapering, I would have to get more and start over because they would pee or poop everywhere before I could get their diapers on.

Trying to find preemie-sized diapers proved to be an exhausting chore. My husband frantically searched specialty stores, hospital gift shops and discount stores for four or five days before finally finding them at a neighborhood grocery store. And good grief, they were expensive—$10.99 for one package! I thought that was a bit much, especially when there were only twenty diapers in a package, and my girls were going through twenty to forty diapers a day.

The nurses at the hospital told us we could use newborn diapers on the twins, but my girls were so small the diapers swallowed them. And when I folded the cloth down it puckered and leaked. I had no choice but to buy preemie size. Of course, Richard cringed every time I'd tell him the girls were almost out of diapers. He'd roll his eyes and say, "Again?"

When it came to bath time, I was the one rolling my eyes. I was nervous because I was concerned about hurting the girls. I absolutely refused to bathe them alone. Richard always helped me at bath time and we always bathed Rebekah and Rachel separately. It was easier and safer that way. Richard and I had bath time down to a science. Our routine reminded me of working on an assembly line.

First, I would get a sponge and the infant bathtub and place them in the kitchen sink. Then I would get one of the girls, place her in a bounce seat and put her in an area where she would be directly in my view while her sister was in the tub. Meanwhile, Richard would undress the other baby and place her in the infant bathtub. At this point, one of the girls would start crying—usually the one not getting washed.

Richard and I would try to entertain the crying baby by making funny faces at her or singing while bathing the other baby at the same time. When we finished giving one baby a bath, I would dry her, dress her and place her in the bounce seat her sister had been in, while Richard took the other baby out and put her in the bathtub. Then we would start the process all over again without missing a beat—nothing like a game of trading places.

While it is a huge challenge caring for two babies, my husband and I have had nothing but blessings. Our twins add so much joy to our lives. And every day is an adventure. Our friends sometimes say, "I don't know how you do it." The truth is, we wouldn't know how to—and wouldn't want to—live our lives any differently. When we consider the fact that we were blessed with two healthy, happy, beautiful babies we wouldn't have it any other way.

Sarah's Savvy Strategies

- Learn to let go of things you cannot control.
- Take charge of things you can control.
- Love each child for the individual she is, and meet her needs as that individual.

Baby Balance—
The Good Mother Myth

Of course Sarah was terrified when she had to take her babies home! New-mother doubts are not only common, but realistic, as was mentioned in Shirley's story. You cannot expect to feel completely confident about something you have never done before. But Sarah not only had to learn to be a mother, she had to do so while juggling two babies—twice the physical work, twice the cries and cues to figure out, twice the time involved, twice the babies to love. Though she was surprised by this news, in some ways she had been mentally preparing for it since her father's prediction. She may have been imagining it in her head, a bit of a dress rehearsal for the real event. Then, when it actually happened that way, she was ready to take it on. She traveled the path successfully—a moral for all those new mothers out there, whether with one baby or more. You, too, can do it!

CAUTION
GOOD MOTHER
MYTHS AHEAD

- Good mothers get their babies to sleep through the night.
- Good mothers can control their babies.
- Babies sleep twenty hours per day.

Exploring Good Mother Myths

Myths rear their ugly heads again in Sarah's story. This time, the myths are about sleep, control and being a good mother. Have you heard the one about babies sleeping twenty hours a day? This myth leads us to expect that this sweet little baby won't require much from mom—she will be too busy sawing logs! Do you hear a chuckle, or even a guffaw in the background? That is the voice of most experienced moms laughing out loud. Sarah believed that one at first, too. She desperately wanted those babies to sleep at night. But as often happens, the babies had their days and nights turned around. Sarah and Richard then fell prey to the myth of control.

Many new parents do everything in the "right" order. They finish school, establish their work life, get married, set up housekeeping—all in preparation for starting a family. Having executed all these tasks the way society recommends, they have a sense of control over their world. They think they can make things happen the way that they want them to. Then *boom,* the baby comes along, and the myth of control crumbles. Parents discover that the baby is a person in his own right, with preferences, a temper and a will of his own. And they cannot exert the control over the baby that they imagined they could! Sarah and Richard could not *make* their babies sleep. They could only set up the circumstances to encourage the girls to sleep when they were tired.

Truths About Babies and Sleep

This is a general truth: Babies eat, sleep, poop and cry pretty much when they want to. They cannot control themselves much, and parents control them even less. Babies do get tired and need to sleep, and a developmental task is to learn to put themselves to sleep. Parents can set up the household to encourage sleep, and then watch for the signs that baby is nearing sleep. To encourage sleep, follow these suggestions:

- Have a quiet place for baby away from the noise of the household. Everything is stimulating for a baby, and too much stimulation may interfere with the baby's ability to unwind and let sleep come. Keeping baby in the same room as the TV or radio or even softly talking parents can interfere with this process.
- Help baby settle down by rocking or feeding her, or by giving her something to suck, such as a pacifier.
- Don't always wait for the baby to fall asleep before laying her down. She will learn to put herself to sleep if she is laid in her bed when she is drowsy. When she is ready to sleep, she may give you one or more of the following signals: rubbing her eyes; fluttering her eyelids as she is nodding off; or even crying in a soft monotone that sounds like *eh, eh, eh.*
- Avoid too much stimulation at one time. Rocking, singing *and* massage may simply raise baby's level of arousal rather than putting her to sleep.

- Understand that once asleep, your baby will sleep in natural cycles of light sleep alternating with deep sleep. If she has fallen asleep in your arms and you wish to lay her down, try waiting twenty minutes until she is in a deep-sleep phase. She will be less likely to wake up when you lay her down.
- Don't immediately whisk your baby out of her crib if she fusses slightly when she moves into a lighter stage of sleep. If you leave her for just a few moments, she may take herself back into a deeper sleep.

Sleeping through the night is an essential skill for the survival of you and your baby. It is a task each baby has to learn, with the parents' help. This task involves learning to calm herself, finding ways to go deeply asleep other than nursing and learning to go back to sleep before fully awake. As each piece falls into place, your baby will soon be sleeping through the night—and you want to encourage that milestone! If you want more information on this approach to baby's sleep, read *The Self-Calmed Baby* by William Sammons, M.D.

Truths About Parental Control

Sarah's difficulty in orchestrating sleep for Rachel and Rebekah left her feeling like a bad mother. Not being able to control something over which you have no control does not make you a bad mother! Becoming a parent means adjusting to the idea that there are many things you cannot control in your child's life. Kids get viruses in even the cleanest households.

They fall and skin their knees. They put on a T-ball helmet and end up with head lice as a result. They get substandard teachers in school—even in the best schools. Other kids hurt their feelings.

All parents can do is protect their children to the best of their ability—and then support them through the tough parts. Parents can hug and kiss their children, assure them they are loved and tell them they will survive the tougher times. Parents cannot, however, control every aspect of their children's lives. Sarah let go of the sleep issue, and of some of the household tasks, and began sleeping when the babies slept. Then she felt much better.

Sarah also faced the challenge of trying to treat her babies "equally." All parents of more than one child must come to terms with this issue. Whether parents of twins or of one older child and one younger child, parents have to sort out what each child is like as a unique individual—that is, what that child's inherent needs, strengths, quirks and lovable pieces are. It's impossible to treat two children completely equally, as Sarah realized with her babies. You cannot even *love* them equally—you have to love them for who they are. Even twins! In *Siblings Without Rivalry,* Adele Faber and Elaine Mazlish assert that parents cannot "love each one best," so they can only love each one for who they are. You *can* meet each child's needs to the best of your ability, but remember which need goes with which child. That is how parents can not only treat children fairly and equitably, but decrease the amount of competition between siblings.

When each child is assured of her mom's love and devotion to her unique needs, the feeling of losing out to a sister or brother is lessened. Sarah discovered this with time. After all, if Rachel wanted to play with the singing dinosaur, but Rebekah preferred the squeaking pink pig, is there any point in making sure Rebekah has equal time with the dinosaur? That is what being a good mother is about: distinguishing each child's needs and working to meet them in the best way possible.

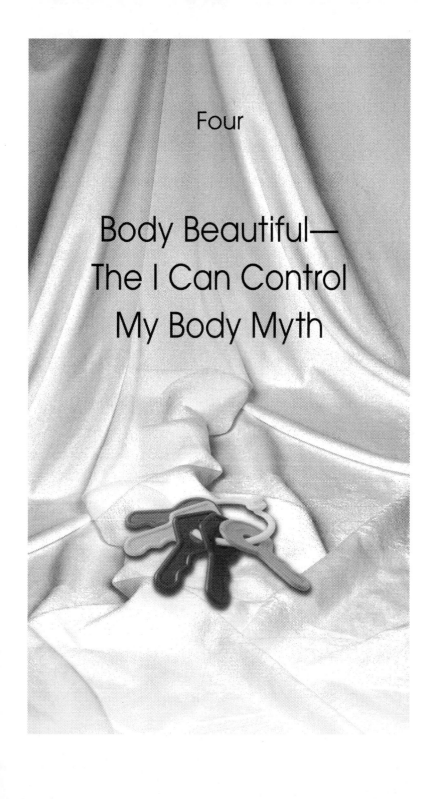

Four

Body Beautiful—
The I Can Control
My Body Myth

I Can Control My Body— Myth or Reality?

Maybe you wanted to get pregnant at just the right time, so the baby's birth would coincide with other life events. Or maybe you wanted the birth to go exactly according to your detailed birth plan. And of course you want those baby pounds off before that big wedding for your sister. How easy is all this to achieve? Most of the time, the reality is that we control our bodies to a limited extent. Pregnancy and childbirth are often the first experience we have with facing the limits to our control of our bodies.

My name is Casey Priest.
I am a public relations director at a
retail store, and I am the proud mother
of a beautiful little boy.

Baby's Name: _Wyatt Cornett_

Date of Birth: _February 15, 2000_

Time of Birth: _12:19 A.M._

Weight: _7 pounds, 11 ounces_

Length: _19¼ inches_

After I found out I was pregnant, I drove straight to Taco Bell. I was thinking, *I've got to eat. I've got to eat.* And I did. I gained forty pounds during my pregnancy. I didn't worry too much about the weight initially because I just knew that after I had my baby the extra pounds would roll off my body like water off a duck's back. And I would jump back into the cute little jeans I had worn before I was pregnant.

I went into labor on Valentine's Day while sitting at my desk at the office. I felt a sharp pang in my stomach, and I knew right away it was a contraction. I remember thinking how exciting it

> *One day I caught a glimpse of myself in the mirror, and I freaked out. I did not like my reflection at all. I felt frumpy, gross and huge.*
>
> —CASEY PRIEST

would be to have my baby on the day set aside to honor love, but that was not to be. One of my colleagues drove me home and before I could relax my water broke. My husband and I were thrilled. We moved quickly, grabbing my luggage and the keys to the car. By the time we arrived at the hospital, I had dilated five centimeters and was progressing rapidly.

When it was time to push I did it with all my might, but my baby wouldn't come out. He somehow managed to lodge under my pelvic bone, and I had to have an emergency C-section. That scared me at first because my husband and I had not considered the possibility of having emergency surgery. But I calmed down as I prepared for the operation. In fact, when my husband changed into a pair of scrubs I smiled and blurted, "You look so cute. You should be on a soap opera."

Less than an hour later, my adorable baby boy was born, the day after Valentine's Day. I remember looking at Wyatt and falling head over heels in love with him. It was as if I had been shot with Cupid's arrow. Like magic, I understood right away what mothers mean when they say, "Babies offer instant love that is totally unconditional." It was the best feeling in the world.

Wyatt and I bonded right away. He was such a good baby. He wasn't fussy. He didn't cry a lot. And he latched on immediately. Everything was perfect. My husband slept on an uncomfortable sofa next to my hospital bed, and he helped me feed and care for Wyatt. I was pleasantly shocked by how everything seemed to click. I was worried about mothering initially because I am an only child, and I had never been around a lot of babies. Mothering, however, was better than I had dreamed it would be—at first.

Unfortunately, when I got home from the hospital my joy gave way to pain and tears. One day I caught a glimpse of myself in the mirror, and I freaked out. I did not like my reflection at all. I felt frumpy, gross and huge. My face was puffy, my arms were flabby and I still looked like I was at least four months pregnant. I was devastated by my self-evaluation and certainly felt less than attractive. Worse, I no longer felt like I had control of my body and its functions. Milk flowed from my breasts like water from a faucet. It unnerved me that I was producing milk all the time—even when I wasn't nursing my baby. I ended up putting extra nursing pads in my bra in an attempt to absorb the overflow. I was taken aback by my body's transformation. To me, the changes were like something out of a science fiction movie.

One day, one of my girlfriends came over to see me. I made sure everything was perfect for our visit. Wyatt was sleeping, I had plenty of snacks and everything was under control. After talking with my friend for about an hour, I happened to glance down at the front of my shirt and it was soaking wet. It was covered with breast milk. I was so shocked and embarrassed I cried. My girlfriend was very understanding and tried to be cute about the whole thing, but I was an emotional wreck. My shoulders sagged under the weight of the tremendous stress.

My mother-in-law was the first to recognize I was surrendering to pressure. Being a mother of three, it was easy for her to pick up on telltale signs. She offered to watch Wyatt and encouraged me to treat myself to something special. I took her up on the offer and decided to get a new haircut. That was the first step toward changing my image and making my body beautiful again.

Excited, I went to a new salon, sat in the stylist's chair and told him I was a new mom and I wanted something fresh and cute. He ran his fingers through my velvety smooth hair, made a few suggestions and then started to cut my wispy locks. As I watched my hair fall to the floor, I couldn't wait to see my new hairdo. I closed my eyes and tried to imagine what I would look like. It didn't take long before the suspense came to an end. Feeling confident and pleased with the job he had done, the stylist handed me a small mirror expecting instant approval.

When I looked into its round face and saw my hair I burst into tears. It was the most awful haircut I had ever gotten. My hair was uneven—long in the front and short in the back. It looked like a bad eighties asymmetrical cut. I sobbed hysterically and yelled, "I can't believe you did this to me." Terribly upset, I jumped out of the black swivel chair and went home. My husband and mother-in-law loved my new 'do and thought it was cute. My baby certainly didn't complain, but I did. I hated my new look with a burning passion.

I was at a point where I didn't like anything about my hair or my body. The strange thing was no one thought I was unattractive except me. While I valued my family's and friends' opinions, what was in *my* mind was all that mattered. I was extremely frustrated because I didn't like my image or how I felt about myself. And the prevailing fact that I could no longer wear any of my pre-pregnancy clothes added insult to injury.

Determined to feel better about myself, I packed up four-week-old Wyatt and my mother-in-law and we all went on an aggressive shopping spree. I wanted something to lift my spirits and put me in a better frame of mine. Unfortunately, that wasn't something that could be bought off a store shelf. So I went on a mission to buy the next best thing: hip, fashionable clothes—clothes I could feel good in and look absolutely fabulous wearing.

I had always prided myself on having a thin upper body, and I thought it was still kind of thin after Wyatt was born. Accentuating my positive feature became my immediate goal. Within minutes, I found a beautiful cotton shirt hanging on a rack in a size medium. I held it against my chest as I admired it. My mother-in-law looked at me in disbelief, shook her head from side to side, and murmured, "I think you need a large." I flew into a tirade. "I have never bought a large shirt in my life. And I am not going to buy one now," I blurted. "I have always been a small. I'm compromising by buying a medium. Don't tell me I need to get a large," I mumbled under my breath. I absolutely refused to purchase the large shirt.

The teenage cashier smiled and asked if I had found everything okay before she rang up the medium-sized shirt. "Yes, I did," I answered without a hint of doubt about the size I was buying. As I waited patiently for the teen to bag my purchase, guilt settled in. I felt badly for yelling at my mother-in-law for suggesting I purchase a large shirt. In retrospect, I know she was only trying to help. And she was right. I needed a large-sized shirt, but I didn't care. I bought a medium one instead and wore it proudly. I'm sure I looked funnier than a clown in a traveling circus, but that shirt made me feel better about myself—at least for a while.

My relationship with my husband changed in the midst of the turmoil surrounding my struggle with my body. I no longer felt sexual or romantic. And I cringed at the thought of making love. Not because I didn't find my husband attractive or desirable—I did. I just felt like my body was devoted to my baby. I was breastfeeding Wyatt several times a day and tending to his every need. My husband's attitude was like, "When is this going to get better?" I couldn't answer that question. All I could do was ask for patience—which he granted without hesitation.

It took about five months for me to start feeling good about my body again. A defining moment arrived when I decided to go on a strict diet. I changed my eating habits, counted calories and developed an exercise routine that included taking Wyatt with me for long walks in his stroller. Perhaps more importantly, I began to realize my body was still beautiful and sexual—probably more so since I had become a mother.

Realizing that made it easier for me to reach out to my husband again. A turning point for us happened one day when I came home from work. I ran straight to Wyatt who was nestled in my husband's arms and gave him a big kiss. I totally ignored my husband who looked at me, smiled and said, "When am I going to get some of those kisses again?" That pointed question made me realize how much I had been neglecting him, and it was time I stopped.

As hard as it was to do, my husband and I took a vacation without Wyatt. He was almost six months old, and I was no longer breast-feeding him. We left Wyatt with my parents and went to San Francisco where we found romance again. My husband and I toured the wine country and shared conversations that did not focus solely on our baby, but rather on us spending more time together. It was the best thing we ever did. Of course, Wyatt was never out of our thoughts. We called to check on him every day—three or four times a day.

When my husband and I returned home from our trip, I began to feel even more comfortable with my body. When I looked in the mirror I wasn't disappointed. I was happy because I liked my reflection. I could wear my old jeans again. And I was in control of my body!

Casey's Savvy Strategies

- Make time for your partner, sexually and socially.
- Accentuate your best features with new clothes or hairstyles.
- Control what you can, with a healthy diet and exercise.

Body Beautiful—
The I Can Control My Body Myth

When a woman has a baby, she faces enormous changes within herself: how she views herself as a person, how she views her physical body, how she views the control she has over the world. Casey's story illustrates some powerful changes in one woman's view of her physical and sexual selves as she became a mother.

Watching her body change in remarkable ways over the nine months of pregnancy, a woman may find herself overwhelmed with feelings about whether she still "fits" in that body. A reaction of "Who does this body belong to, anyway?" is common, as Casey describes with her response to her postpartum body in the mirror.

At no other time in a person's life do bodily changes happen so dramatically and rapidly—so of course these changes are hard to get used to. The expectant mother is also torn between competing concerns: maintaining control of her body/figure and providing sustenance for the growing baby inside. Many women are even relieved to get a respite from watching their figures—in fact, eating for two sounds like such fun. As she watches her body morph into that of a pregnant woman's, however, the expectant mom may come face-to-face with a new reality: She can't "control" her body the way she did in the past. For instance, before pregnancy, she may have believed she could control her weight at will: If she watched what she ate, cut back on the sweets and increased the aerobics, she could get back in those size-7 jeans in no time. Pregnancy soon puts an end to this variation on the "control" myth.

As many women discover through the morning sickness of early pregnancy and the heartburn and sleeplessness of later pregnancy, such bodily control is an illusion. At some point during pregnancy, hormonal changes and challenges override a woman's ability to "control" her body. Casey voices this reality with her comments about having a cesarean section. Few women who hear about the C-section rate in childbirth classes believe it will happen to them, because they believe they have this mythical mastery over all bodily processes.

After childbirth, Casey was bound and determined to regain control of her body again, too—she would *not* succumb to being a woman who needed a "large" shirt. Casey is not unique in her feelings. In a study by Jane Weaver and Jane Ussher at University College, London, new mothers asserted that their lives had changed when they became mothers, but they had *not* changed as people. Each of these women was quite firm that her "core self" was intact. She may have looked or seemed different to others, but her self-perception had not been altered by motherhood.

The researchers suggested that all the changes in a new mother's life threaten her view of herself and consequently her self-esteem. If a new mother is unsure about herself, and expresses her uncertainty, she may fear that she will be viewed as less valuable. By maintaining that she is still the same person inside, the new mom can preserve her self-esteem. Casey is a good example of this process in action. She valued her "thin upper body." It was one of the reasons she felt good about herself, so she refused to give up that view of herself; to do so might mean she was less valuable.

A new mother's changing feelings about her body, and her lack of comfort with her dual role as mom and sexual partner, are also clearly spelled out in Casey's story. Many new mothers experience a lack of sexual feelings. After all, if your body does not feel like your own, or look like your own, how can you trust that it will respond sexually in the same way it used to? Fatigue also plays a large role in lack of sexual interest in most new mothers. You are drained from feeding, walking, rocking and lifting your baby. You are in close physical contact with another human being, your newborn, for much of the day, especially if you are breastfeeding. Just as people in wheelchairs experience a craving for physical contact that is called "skin hunger," new mothers may crave freedom *from contact,* or from a "skin overload."

Anne Woollett and Mel Parr of the Psychology Department of the University of East London

Why Sex Is Last on the List for Many New Moms

- Fatigue/exhaustion
- Skin overload (unending physical contact with baby)
- Changing hormones
- Ideas about motherhood and sex being incompatible
- Chore overload
- Lack of comfort with a changed body
- Lack of time for self
- Lack of nurturing from others
- Overwhelming feelings about new role and responsibilities

studied men and women across several years as they adjusted to parenthood. When speaking of sex, the new mothers reported, "I am just not interested anymore. I am tired. I just want space around me in the bed. [Sex] is the last thing on my mind." New mothers often use up all the emotional and physical nurturing that they have in them while caring for their infants, and by bedtime many new moms may be "running on empty." The last thing on their minds is giving—sexually or otherwise—to their partner. With a day so full of physical contact and taking care of the needs of another, the last thing a new mother may want to hear is that her partner has physical needs, too. Poor Dad.

Some women (and men) even carry taboos in their heads about sex and mothers. That adolescent notion that mothers do *not* have sex dies hard. After all, few of us are comfortable acknowledging, as we begin to feel sexual in the teen years, that our parents could feel the same way—eeuugh! And these feelings sometimes carry over into new parenthood and color our expectations about how we should feel about sex now that we are mothers. Even if these feelings are not active, a woman may simply feel torn between the two roles of spouse and mother. As one woman told Anne Woollett and Mel Parr: "As a mother, I cannot simply switch the baby off."

Finally, many new mothers lose interest in their sex life with their partner because of general overload. The new mom's brain may be so preoccupied with remembering feeding times, learning her baby's cries and working to feel like a mother, that she cannot even think about sex. Sure, it was fun before. It may have been a very satisfying part of the couple's relationship, but now the new mom's life is full of new tasks and new information. She is simply too absorbed in being a mother.

Restoring Your Love Life

Couples can use a variety of strategies to get their sex life back on track after the birth of a baby. Consider one of these ideas for making sexual intimacy a realistic priority:

- Designate one night each week for physical closeness. If you know ahead of time that you want to be able to give sexually to your partner on a specific evening, you can prepare in advance.
- Take an afternoon nap on the designated day when the baby is sleeping, or get extra help from a friend or relative that day.
- That evening, ask your partner to take an extra tour of duty with the baby, bathing him or giving the final feeding while you soak in the tub or listen to some relaxing music.
- When the baby is in bed for the night, you and your spouse can devote some time to physical closeness. This does not have to be sexual at first, particularly if you're not comfortable with that. You can focus on massage or cuddling if that is less demanding.
- You and your spouse may also need to be creative about your timing. For example, your baby's weekend nap times may make for better "couple time" because the new mom is much less fatigued.

This approach to intimacy may lack the spontaneity you enjoyed pre-motherhood, but the fact that with a plan like this sex actually can happen may outweigh that loss.

Just as Donna found her relationships with family and friends changing, becoming a mother also changes a couple's relationship. Before becoming parents, couples can make each other a priority. They have time to devote to each other. The connection between them is a straight line, with give and take, and no other parties intervening. Once the baby arrives, the relationship has to be revised, and often turns into a triangle.

The partners can still relate to each other directly but often relate only through the baby. What did the baby do today? Usually they are both interested in this topic. Talk of the baby's antics, troubles and developments rules the household for awhile. This is partly because of the novelty of the baby, partly because of the time-consuming nature of the baby. Often the new mom has little time for her other interests so this is what she has to talk about.

The new father may find himself tired of his partner's single-mindedness. He wants his old wife back—the one who could argue politics, or solve the crossword puzzle with him, or stay awake for the late show. Or, as in Casey's story, the one who provided needed kisses. New moms often forget, when faced with a helpless new baby, that their partners have needs, too. They have sexual needs, of course, but also needs to talk and be listened to and get hugs and kisses.

Babies are good at getting their needs met. They scream and wail and generally command attention from all those in the vicinity. Partners may need to be tactful about their needs, and how they miss the old ways of interacting. Casey's husband did this quite well, and so conflict was avoided.

Restoring Your Couple Connection

Arguments about these issues are quite common among new parents. Each may feel like he or she made a bigger sacrifice. He feels his needs are not being met; she feels the most deprived or exhausted. At times like these, it helps to remember that both partners are "in it together." It is hard adjusting to the demands of a new baby for both parents. Both may be tired; both make sacrifices. Both have to make efforts to maintain the couple relationship.

Structuring time to spend together needs to be a priority. A long weekend away, as Casey and her spouse had, can be a wonderful way to renew the sense of "we are a couple, and we are important to each other," not just parents together. But smaller bits of time are equally important for maintaining a sense of balance between the new roles and the old patterns.

- Set aside time to sit together on the couch each evening and share good and bad points from each person's day.
- Arrange a weekly date to have coffee or dinner together after the baby is in bed, or watch a video or favorite TV program.
- Make a ritual out of the morning parting or evening return by making sure hugs or a greeting such as "glad you're home" are exchanged.

- Remember that you had this baby because you liked things about each other. Focus on those things and remind yourself and your partner why you are in this together.

With a little effort, and the use of these rituals, the balance in the relationship often returns with ease.

Casey's story reminds us that all of these feelings about changing bodies, changing sexuality and changing relationships are completely normal and part of the adjustment to motherhood. The new mother learns to like her body again, to regain some control over it. And as this happens, and as she gets a bit more rest and feels less drained, she becomes more comfortable with her sexual side. New motherhood is so all-absorbing, it often takes several months before the new mom feels like the old parts of herself, such as sexuality, coexist with the new mother parts. The encouraging news is, it will happen!

Five

Baby Connection—
The Bonding Myths

Instant Bonding: Myth or Reality?

Love at first sight? You may have read tales of mothers who swooned with love for their wrinkled, messy baby on the delivery table. Mothers who felt this way seem to love to tell these tales. But the reality is that there are as many different ways and timetables for mother and baby to connect as there are moms and babies. Please do not despair if your bonding with your baby does not fit the "instant bonding" criteria. Nearly 100 percent of moms find that they are head over heels in love by the time the baby is three months old.

My name is Elizabeth Gambrell. I am an attorney and the proud mother of a beautiful little girl.

Baby's Name: *Eleanor Anne*

Date of Birth: *October 19, 1999*

Time of Birth: *9:06 A.M.*

Weight: *7 pounds*

Length: *20 inches*

razy. C-r-a-z-y. That's how I felt when I had my baby—like I had lost my mind. I figured I must have gone off the deep end because when my beautiful baby girl was born I did not have a reaction toward her. I wasn't very excited. I didn't cry. And I didn't feel like a mother. That was very disappointing. And the emptiness left me feeling overwhelmed with tremendous guilt. I was frazzled and frightened, and I wondered why I didn't feel instant love for my baby.

Before Eleanor was born, several mothers told me the birth of a child was the most wonderful thing in the world, and it is, but when my doctor

> *. . . when my doctor gave me my baby I did not feel connected to her.*
>
> —ELIZABETH GAMBRELL

gave me my baby I did not feel connected to her. I just thought, *Oh, here's a little baby who I don't know and who is going to take over my life.* I was more excited when I saw my baby on a sonogram moving around in my stomach than I was when she was born. That pained me—and was far beyond my comprehension.

I felt like my emotions were going haywire. I was sinking— and sinking fast. And no matter how hard I tried I couldn't stop what was happening to me. This downward effect started before I left the hospital. I was nursing Eleanor, and I don't know if it was the pain medication I was taking or my hormones, but I suddenly felt very nervous and stressed. I started having panic attacks.

At the time, I thought I was having a negative reaction to medication I was taking for pain. My doctor changed the prescription, but that did not solve my problem. The second night at the hospital, I was still panicky and jittery, and I could not sleep. I don't know why sleep eluded me, but it did. I was taken aback because Eleanor was a great baby. She latched on right away, she did not cry much and she was sleeping four to six hours every night. But no matter how hard I tried I could not doze off.

The insomnia continued after I brought Eleanor home from the hospital. I laid awake in bed for hours trying desperately to fall asleep, but to no avail. My mother was visiting at the time and helping me care for my baby. She even slept in the nursery with Eleanor so that I could rest. My mom was terrific. I can still hear her voice brimming with emotion, "Elizabeth, you know I will be with the baby. If she needs anything I will be right there. You don't have to worry. Now close your eyes and go to sleep."

I felt very comfortable with my mother being with me, and I knew she was doing an excellent job caring for my baby, but no matter how hard I tried I just couldn't nod off. I cried uncontrollably every day, and I was so exhausted. It was a very scary situation for me because I was so fatigued and stressed. Feeling completely desperate, I called my doctor and got a prescription for sleeping pills, but I was afraid to take them. I was nursing, and I didn't want to hurt Eleanor. So I cut each tablet into fourths and took a quarter of the recommended dose.

The medicine helped a little, but then I became nervous about taking it. I was losing so much sleep that my mind started playing tricks on me. I began to think every bad thought I had would become reality. For example, I thought if I took the sleeping pills as prescribed I would fall into a deep sleep, and Eleanor would starve because no one would be able to wake me to nurse her. I was so concerned my baby was going to starve that I couldn't relax.

I was surprised by my behavior because I felt great during my pregnancy. It was easy. My delivery was easy. And I never had a problem sleeping before. The sleepless pattern went on for about two weeks. It was the longest and worst time of my life. Then one day, as quick as a snap of a finger, I fell asleep. My husband told me I was going to look back on the situation and laugh. Well, I can talk about it, but I still can't laugh because it was such a difficult time.

Although I got past my inability to sleep, my mind was still caught up in an unrelenting storm. I couldn't stand the darkness. I know that sounds strange, but I had to have light—all the time. Eleanor was born in October—the month daylight savings time ends and it gets dark early. Every time day gave way to night, I got depressed. I got so down I turned on every light in the house, every night, because I felt like everything was closing in on me. It was like having claustrophobia. My mother kept telling me, "Elizabeth, it always gets dark early this time of year. You know that. It is a very normal thing." Of course I knew that, but my mind was doing things that were anything but normal.

I was very frightened because I didn't recognize the woman I had become. Still, I knew that in order to survive in my new world I would have to make adjustments and accept my new lot in life. That wasn't easy to do. When Eleanor was born, everything I knew and was familiar with was different—nothing was the same. I wasn't the same. I remember wanting desperately to go back to the way things were before I had my baby, because I couldn't cope with my new life. I wanted to go back to work where it was peaceful and quiet. I wanted to get into my car without a baby and take long drives. I wanted to sit down in the family room and watch football games with my husband. I wanted my old life back, plain and simple, because my new one did not feel comfortable.

After about three months, I started to settle down. A sense of peace and an unfamiliar feeling of normalcy returned to my life and enfolded me like a soft wool blanket. I began to relax, get over my fears and get the hang of mothering. As I bask in sunshine now, I realize having a baby is a huge, life-changing experience. While it was difficult for me to adjust initially, I found my way out of the path of the storm. I feel calm now. And when I look at Eleanor, my little sweet pea, I feel very connected to her in every way. We are incredibly close. I love everything about my baby—her smile, her touch and her unconditional love.

Elizabeth's Savvy Strategies

- Know that there is nothing wrong with you if your new life isn't wonderful.
- Ask for help—whether a break, a nap, laundry folded or medication to sleep.

The analysis of Elizabeth's story and her issues surrounding bonding follows Andrea Thompson's story. Andrea's experience illustrates another perspective on the attachment between mother and baby.

My name is Andrea Thompson.
*I am a former star of **NYPD Blue**, a former*
***CNN Headline News** anchor and the proud*
mother of a beautiful little boy.

Baby's Name: _Alec Daniel_

Date of Birth: _September 30, 1992_

Time of Birth: _9:43 P.M._

Weight: _7 pounds_

Length: _19½ inches_

was alone when my baby was born. His father walked out on me when I was two months pregnant. He said he couldn't handle being a father, being responsible, being committed to me, being committed to our baby. That was an incredible blow. Deeply wounded, I was determined to have my baby and be the best mother I could be.

Part of that meant earning a living to support me and my baby. I worked feverishly throughout my pregnancy. There aren't a lot of jobs on the silver screen for women in Hollywood—especially pregnant women. I was basically doing voice-over work. In fact, I was working when I went into labor. It was a warm sunny Tuesday afternoon—somewhat typical of Los Angeles weather. I started having labor pains during my first voice-over booking that day. I managed to complete the job and move on to my second one. By that time the labor pains

> *I just knew my baby and I were going to die. I asked for a priest to give us our last rites.*
>
> —ANDREA THOMPSON

were twenty minutes apart. I had to stop recording every now and again to catch my breath, but I managed to get everything done.

When it was over I gathered my personal belongings, jumped into my car and drove to the hospital. I pulled in front of the facility, dropped off my luggage, parked my car in long-term parking and walked three blocks back to the hospital and registered. Although I was taken to the delivery room immediately, things weren't progressing quickly so my doctor gave me medicine to accelerate the labor. By this time the contractions were painful beyond belief.

Labor went on for thirty hours. During that time, my baby and I came very close to dying. The umbilical cord was wrapped around his neck, and the placenta, the organ that provided him nourishment, had somehow detached from the wall of my uterus and come out—cutting off my baby's oxygen supply. We were in severe distress. My blood pressure was dropping rapidly, hovering at sixty over forty. The team of doctors knew we were in an emergency situation, but they couldn't do a cesarean section because it was clearly too risky. My blood pressure was simply too low. Any drop in pressure could have caused me to have a low-end stroke.

The medical staff tried frantically to save me and my baby. My blood pressure was still very low. I remember someone putting an oxygen mask on my face, a blood pressure cuff on my arm and heart-monitor leads on my chest. Hooked up to all that equipment, I just knew my baby and I were going to die. I asked for a priest to give us our last rites.

That was important to me. I was raised strictly Catholic. I attended Mass every morning from the time I was six years old. I went to confession twice a week. And I said my rosary every night on my knees beside my bed until I was fifteen. That's when I ran away from my religion. I completely rejected it. I thought I had abandoned that part of my life, until I saw death staring me in the face—waiting patiently to claim my life and the life of my unborn child. I don't know why, but I didn't panic. I simply reached out to my religion and took comfort in its embrace.

With the priest standing at my bedside I prayed and asked to be forgiven for all my sins. The moment I felt like the end was near I made it clear to my doctors that if they could save either of us, they should save my baby. I knew my family members would take care of him. I had made arrangements with them beforehand. I know that may sound strange, but I'm a very realistic person. Having grown up surrounded by people in the medical field—my stepfather was a doctor, one of my brothers is a doctor, another brother is a hospital administrator and my mother is a nurse—I knew the risks involved with childbirth.

So I made sure my will, trust and insurance were in order. I also wrote letters to the people in my family that I love and put them in my safe deposit box. But the best thing I did beforehand was make a videotape for my baby just in case I didn't make it through delivery. I set up my camera, looked into its lens and just talked to him while he was in my womb.

I had already named my baby. I was three months pregnant when I decided what to call him. I was in the kitchen making dinner and I said to myself, *This is a boy, and his name is Alec.* I don't know how I knew that. I just knew. At any rate, I said, "Alec, you are the best thing that has ever happened in my life. I don't feel like I ever really got it until you came along. I don't feel like I actually grew up until I knew you were coming into my life. I love you."

Even though I had prepared for the worst, I never imagined the two of us—my baby and I—would be fighting for our lives. I wasn't afraid of what was happening, and I wasn't afraid of dying. I had a great sense of peace about it. It was sort of like being underwater.

I remember being able to hear my breathing and feel my heart beating. I felt very sleepy and heavy. On an intellectual level I knew my life was slipping away, but again I felt at peace because I knew I had reached out to everyone I cared for and everyone I had had an argument with to make amends. I knew I wasn't leaving any loose ends behind. And I knew my baby would be cared for.

Realizing that, there was only one thing left for me to do. I closed my eyes, and I prayed. The next thing I knew, my doctor was placing a beautiful, healthy little baby boy on my chest. When I saw my precious baby I said, "Hello, Alec." And he opened his eyes and just gave kind of a sigh. Before I even thought about it I licked his head which was still covered with birth matter. It was the strangest thing I had ever done. It was one of those moments in life that takes you back to the primal beginnings of mankind.

Oh, how I love Alec. I knew from the moment I discovered I was pregnant that I would always love and protect him. As I looked at Alec that very moment, in total amazement, and I thought about all that we had gone through, especially during delivery, I realized it was worth it. It was so worth it. And if I had died during birth, that would have been worth it too because my son is the greatest thing that has ever happened to me.

Andrea's Savvy Strategies

- Anticipate the worst and prepare for every possibility. This does not mean you need to be fearful, just practical.
- Explore how faith can be a valuable aid to your life as a parent.

Bonding with Baby

Cultural myths around the process of becoming a mother are powerful. In Elizabeth's story, the cultural myth of "instant bonding" is explored, together with the idea that the process is instantaneous and absolute. In the bonding—or "attachment"—myth, either it happens or it doesn't. There is no allowance for the degrees of connection that grow between parent and child.

The truth is that a mother's bonding, or falling in love with her baby, is not subject to hard and fast rules or strict time-tables. Andrea's story illustrates one extreme on the spectrum, while Elizabeth's represents the other end. Andrea perceived that her bonding with Alec took place at the moment of birth, when in reality she had been building to that moment throughout the months of her pregnancy.

Elizabeth's and Andrea's stories point out how each mother and baby has a unique bonding pattern. In Andrea's story, she definitely bonded with her unborn baby. This is just as common as not falling in love fully until the baby is three months old. These variations on the bonding process remind us that there is no one "right" way or time to bond with your baby. What is important is a successful conclusion.

The Reality About the Bonding Process

The myth about "instant bonding," and stories about "falling in love on the delivery table," grew in the 1960s and

1970s as birth practices began to change in this country. Researchers realized that newborns and mothers fared better with immediate contact at birth, with mother and baby awake, rather than having the new mother knocked out and the baby whisked away to a nursery for observation. Health professionals began encouraging, and mothers began demanding, instant contact between mom and baby. Somewhere along the line we translated the importance of this early contact or "attachment" between mom and baby to the theory of a "critical period for bonding."

In the animal world, particularly among fowl such as ducks and geese, there is indeed a critical period for the bonding between parent and offspring. A baby duck attaches to the first thing it sees when it hatches. Whether the baby duck sees a human or a cat or a goose, the duckling believes that that is "mom." And the duckling will follow that creature around until it learns otherwise.

Humans do not have a critical period in this same way. The bond between infant and parent is one that often evolves slowly—not instantaneously on the delivery table or birthing bed. Elizabeth did not feel this "instant" love, and so she was concerned. She felt guilty and thought she might be a failure as a parent. The reality is that the bond between mother and baby grows slowly for most parents, either across the months of pregnancy or during the postpartum months.

How the bond develops is affected by many factors, including family background, how your parents bonded with you, parenting styles, life circumstances, experience with other children and your desire to have a baby in the first place. The physical stress that Elizabeth felt after Eleanor's birth may have hampered the bonding process between them. When a new mother is exhausted or overwhelmed with negative feelings, she simply may not have the energy to focus on much but her recovery.

Often, too, new parents need some reaction from the baby before the bond between them can grow. Until the baby begins to respond with smiles and vocalizations—between eight and twelve weeks of age—many parents feel little connection to their babies. The baby seems simply a damp, fussy lump. When the baby begins to react to the parents, cooing and keeping eye contact for longer periods, the bond grows. When the toddler falls and skins a knee, the bond grows even more. New mothers should keep this process in mind, for that is what the relationship between mother and baby is—a process that takes time, rather than "love at first sight."

The Toll of Falling Hormone Levels

Elizabeth's story again illustrates the power of changing hormones for new mothers. In Donna's story in chapter 2, the positive influence of those hormones was evident. Elizabeth's experience represents the negative side of those changes. The large drops in estrogen, progesterone and prolactin took their toll on Elizabeth's mood. Many women simply weather these changes with not much more than fatigue and some tears.

In a recent study by Miki Bloch, M.D., and colleagues, two

groups of women were compared: one with a history of post-partum depression and one with no history of depression. The women in each group were given a powerful drug often used to treat infertility. This essentially stopped their regular hormone function, putting them into a false menopause. Replacement hormones were then administered to all the women, to bring their hormone levels to a standard pregnancy level. Then the hormones were withdrawn. Women who had a history of postpartum depression became depressed; those with no previous depression were fine. This reaction led researchers to conclude that it is not the rise and fall of hormones in itself that triggers postpartum depression. Rather, some women have brain chemistries that are extremely sensitive to these changes, while other women are fairly resistant to the effects of such changes.

Elizabeth appears to be one of the sensitive women for whom powerful emotional reactions can be triggered. Elizabeth had panic attacks and severe insomnia, which are both fairly common for postpartum depression. Postpartum depression is actually a misnomer, as most women with these problems have much more anxiety, panic and worry than the tearfulness, fatigue and lack of interest usually found in depression.

The fact that Elizabeth became quite bothered by the increasing darkness may be another indication of her sensitive hormonal wiring. Seasonal affective disorder (SAD) is a condition in which people become increasingly depressed as the days get shorter and they are exposed to less sunlight. Melatonin, a brain substance related to serotonin, is influenced by exposure to sunlight. Many women with a history of postpartum depression also show this seasonal variation in susceptibility to depression. As it gets darker, they may feel even more anxious and blue. In addition, they may dislike the nights because of extensive sleep problems. As darkness falls, they are again faced with tossing and turning and lying awake alone.

Coping with Lack of Sleep

Unfortunately, sleep deprivation can be very difficult to ride out. As the new mom gets more tired, chemical changes in her brain may worsen, creating a vicious cycle. Sleep deprivation is, after all, one way prisoners-of-war are tortured. Think about what you would do if you wanted to break down someone's resistance: keep the person awake until he or she is so fatigued he or she cannot think straight. That is what sweet, little eight-pound babies can do to parents.

Unrealistic expectations often haunt new mothers in this arena. New mothers may worry to themselves: *How will I take care of the baby if I only get three hours of sleep? I need my sleep—how will I survive?* They may even think, *If I only could get one good night's sleep, all would be fine.* The reality, however, is that it can take up to twenty-one days of good sleep to recover from sleep deprivation—and what new mother can get twenty-one days of uninterrupted sleep? The new mom may toss and turn, tormenting herself with these thoughts.

What new moms need to do is to take a deep breath and remember that this period does not last long. And no one ever died of sleep deprivation. New moms all recover eventually. In the meantime, a new mother can lie down and rest or sleep whenever her baby sleeps. Resting can be just as helpful as actual sleep. Short-term use of sleep aids is usually not harmful. Having new dads or other relatives help with occasional night feedings is invaluable, as Elizabeth found out. Parents of infants younger than two months need to make sleep a priority, getting sleep through whatever means they can. If that means taking the baby into bed—unless it is a waterbed—and the new mom is comfortable with that, then do it (making sure that the baby has ample room to breathe properly). You can worry about getting the baby to sleep in her own bed, if that is your goal, after she begins to sleep a bit longer through the night. You won't be locked in to having a child in your bed when she is four just because she is in your bed at three months. Remember that your baby will begin to sleep for longer periods of time as she gets older, and your body will begin to adjust to the new sleep patterns you have developed to cope.

Savvy Sleep Tips

- Breathe deeply—it may metabolize the adrenaline that keeps you awake.
- Keep your perspective—a temporary lack of sleep is not fatal.
- Focus on rest versus sleep—it will still renew your tired brain.
- Make sleep a priority for now—do *whatever* works.
- Rely on your partner or relatives to take a night feeding for awhile if that will help you catch up on sleep.
- Avoid alcoholic beverages to induce sleep, as "rebound insomnia" may result.

Constant sleep interruptions may confuse a woman's natural sleep rhythms, and she may need to reset her biological clock. If the new mother's sleep cycle gets completely out of whack, she may have to recondition her body using good sleep habits. More information on these techniques is found in the section on Postpartum Realities later in this book. Repeated lack of sleep can result in memory loss, a weakened immune system, and increased feelings of anxiety, irritability and depression. So if you are having difficulty remembering, or you are worried and cranky most of the time, you can write these symptoms off to the loss of sleep. Reassure yourself that these symptoms will decrease when you are able to sneak in more ZZZZs. Sleep deprivation leads to serious postpartum depression in only a small percentage of new mothers. (For more information about that, see the story of Ruthanne Kern in chapter 14.)

Grieving Loss Without Guilt

Elizabeth was grieving the loss of her old life and battling her guilt over having those negative feelings. It is completely legitimate to feel sad when your life has changed drastically and you cannot engage in activities or see friends that you used to enjoy. Allow yourself to feel sad. If you had to move from a city and could no longer see certain friends, you would feel sad. If you had a back injury and could no longer engage in the horseback riding that you loved, you would grieve.

When you become a mother and have similar feelings of grief, you are entitled to them without guilt. Just because you do not like some of the changes in your life does not mean that you wish your baby away, or that you made a mistake choosing to have a baby. It simply means that you miss the old activities, friends or freedoms. You can still love your baby and find joy in your new life.

A Mother's Love and Sacrifice

It was Andrea's prenatal bonding that paved the way for her thoughts that, given a forced choice, the doctors should "save the baby." The baby Alec was already extremely real to her even before his birth because the attachment process had begun. She was ready to give up her own life for his sake simply because she was certain of his reality as a person. She loved him already, so he was very real to her. Much as in the classic children's tale *The Velveteen Rabbit,* having love for another does make them more real to us. Alec was real to Andrea. She loved him, and she really felt like his mother, even before she saw him.

Since our culture dictates that mothers sacrifice for their children, Andrea was ready to sacrifice for her son. In a research study by Weaver and Ussher, new mothers were accepting of this fact, even when that self-sacrifice came at great personal cost. It is a given for most women: You put your child first. For Andrea, there was no further question—saving him was the natural outgrowth of a mother's love for her child.

Just as factors in the mother's personality or background influence the attachment process, so can these factors affect a new mother's outlook on parenting. Andrea was self-sufficient and realistic by nature. She was extremely practical and prepared for the worst. She had learned this growing up surrounded by family members in the medical professions. She knew from their experience that childbirth does not always have perfect outcomes. Being a single parent may also have attuned her to the importance of this practical preparation for parenthood. Her baby only had a mother to count on. Some of us simply can always imagine the worst, and so make sure everything will be handled should that worst occur.

Crisis + Crisis = Extreme Vulnerability

The critical nature of Alec's birth, a true life-or-death situation, meant that Andrea was extremely vulnerable. She was physically vulnerable, of course, but she was also emotionally vulnerable. She wanted this baby badly. She already loved him as a person, not just a concept. With any life change or developmental transition, there is the possibility of heightened emotion and vulnerability.

Andrea was in a *double* crisis situation. Not only was she going through a developmental crisis, i.e., the process of becoming a parent, she was also experiencing a true medical crisis. The lives of Andrea and her son were on the line. Simplistically, when we want something very much and there is a chance we may not get it, we desire it even more. Take that simple fact of human nature and add the intense vulnerability and heightened emotion of a life-or-death crisis, and you can understand how the danger intensified Andrea's love for her baby. Having a baby puts life in perspective because a newborn represents that life goes on. What could possibly outweigh the importance of this new life, so fresh and tender?

Spirituality and the Circle of Life

The possibility of Andrea's life ending as Alec's life was beginning may have heightened Andrea's spiritual focus. When this awareness of new life is contrasted with the threat of death, the "circle of life" becomes very real and up close. Andrea could see that, even if she died during the birth, she would continue in some way on this Earth through Alec.

Faith and spirituality are very important in the adjustment to parenthood for many new mothers, and exposure firsthand to the possibility of death may enhance the new mom's spiritual connections. Andrea made it through the ordeal of Alec's birth in part because of her strong faith. It is likely her spirituality will continue to serve her well as she faces other challenges with Alec, for it obviously is a source of strength for her.

Andrea entered parenthood with a profound awareness of the fragility of life, coupled with intensified faith because she and Alec both made it through the ordeal of birth. Her story reminds us to maintain that awareness: that babies are extraordinary, something to be cherished and enjoyed, above the mundane concerns of our everyday lives, and that faith, when it is present, can be an enriching experience in our lives.

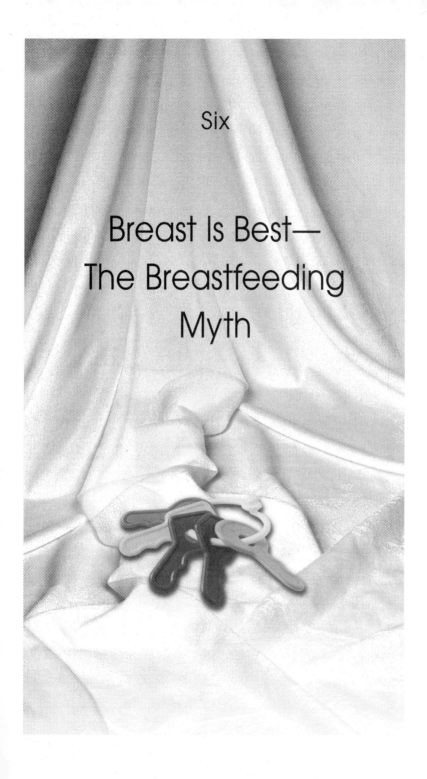

Six

Breast Is Best—
The Breastfeeding
Myth

Breastfeeding—
Sorting Out the Myths

Breastfeeding is how babies have survived since the beginning of humankind, so it must be natural, we think. If it is so natural, then it also must be a breeze. This is true for many women. For many other women, however, breastfeeding is not a breeze. Instead, there is an adjustment period that lasts several weeks, as a new mom's breasts toughen up, the baby masters nursing and mom's milk supply builds and stabilizes.

My name is Deborah Roberts.
I'm a television news correspondent for
ABC News 20/20 *and anchor for* **Lifetime Live.**
I am also the proud mother of
a beautiful little girl.

Baby's Name: _Leila Ruth_

Date of Birth: _November 17, 1998_

Time of Birth: _9:13 A.M._

Weight: _6 pounds, 13 ounces_

Length: _19 inches_

When I was pregnant, everyone—family, friends, even strangers—told me I was having a boy because of the way I was carrying my baby. People would say things like, "You're carrying the baby too low. It's definitely a boy" or "The baby is low and round like a basketball. No question. It's a boy." I heard comments like that so often that I convinced myself that I was, in fact, having a boy. Even though I had a certain number of sonograms during my pregnancy that could reveal the baby's sex, my husband and I decided we didn't want to know the gender of our baby ahead of time. We wanted to have the most wonderful surprise of our lives in the delivery room. And we did.

> *I was surprised by how hard it was to breastfeed Leila. She didn't latch on easily.*
>
> —Deborah Roberts

After being in labor for nineteen hours I had to have a C-section. A few minutes after the procedure started I heard my husband and the doctors marveling over the baby. I couldn't see anything because I was lying flat on my back with a huge cloth in front of my face. I remember thinking, *Hello, hello, I'm back here behind this tent.* Finally the doctor said, "Guess what? It's a girl." I was so shocked I could have fallen off the delivery table. Little did I know that that was the first of many surprises I would have as I settled into motherhood.

When I finally saw Leila—saw her little eyes and her beautiful face—I just burst into tears. It was the most wonderful, exquisite experience I have ever had in my life. To see this little being that I was so desperately waiting to see, and to know she was healthy was absolutely fantastic. Leila is the most precious gift I have ever had handed to me. I was so in awe of her. As I cradled her and watched her, reality started to hit me. I was thinking, *Oh my God. I'm somebody's mother. I'm responsible for somebody's life, her livelihood, her being.* It was scary. I was excited, but I was also terrified.

I also felt a wave of tension when it was time to feed Leila. I was in pain from the surgery, and I was trying to breastfeed her, but it didn't come easily for me. It was a tremendous struggle. I remember thinking, *I have to go home with my baby, and I have to be her mother, but I don't think I can do this.* I was in a slightly depressed state the first few days of mothering, probably the first couple of weeks.

I was surprised by how hard it was to breastfeed Leila. She didn't latch on easily. I had to guide her and help her to my breasts. That required a lot of patience and perseverance on my part, and hers, too. That, coupled with the fact that my breasts were in constant pain didn't help my situation. My breasts hurt, my nipples bled and they were chapped. I know this is graphic, but my breasts really, really hurt. I found myself calling my doctor, lactation specialists, anybody I could think of who could offer expert advice on how to make what is supposed to be such a natural thing work for me and my baby.

I owe a great debt of gratitude to my family and friends. My husband was also very supportive. So were my mom and sister, who came to visit me from out of town on different occasions. They were so warm and so encouraging. When Leila would cry because she was hungry and frustrated, and I would get upset, my sister would be the voice of reason. I remember her telling me repeatedly, "Hey, babies cry. This is a small thing." When Leila was fussy and I'd get bent out of shape, just hearing my mother's tender voice, "Don't worry. Everything will be all right," gave me strength in the midst of crisis and made me feel comfortable.

Several of my girlfriends also came over to help console me. They shared stories about their difficult experiences breastfeeding and how they got through it. Their stories helped me a lot and made me realize all new mothers go through emotional ups and downs and difficulties and that I'm not the first. While it was going on, however, I felt like I was the first mother this had ever happened to and I was the only one who had it so bad.

I'm so thankful I didn't stop trying to breastfeed my baby. We kept trying to nurse until we figured it out. And finally, it happened like magic: Leila latched on, and I just went with the flow. I never put her on a schedule. I went with her needs and fed her when she was hungry. That meant I was chained to the couch a lot—and that made me fall into the hands of depression. I was suffering the blues big time. I remember thinking to myself, *I will never get beyond this point. I will always be wearing a shirt that has spit-up on it and breast milk that has leaked out. I'm just a mess. And I'm always going to look like this.*

But even that changed, and I'm so glad it did. It wasn't long before Leila was sleeping longer and I didn't have to feed her nearly as much. I also learned how to pump milk and store it in bottles for my baby. That gave me a chance to go out to lunch with my husband and friends. And I began to feel like myself again and feel comfortable with my most important role.

When I look at Leila now, I just think, *Oh my God. What a joy! What an absolute miracle!* She is the most beautiful thing I've ever seen. I'm in television news and I often like to tell people my daughter is the best production I have ever done. I just marvel at her existence in our world, I absolutely marvel. When I look back and remember how tough it was breastfeeding Leila, and how down I was, I realize now it was a process. We got through it. Now it's just a memory.

Deborah's Savvy Strategies

- Have patience and persistence if any part of parenthood is harder than you thought it would be.
- Consult the experts—other moms or medical professionals —when faced with difficulties.
- Pay attention to reason: Babies cry, and you will get through it!

Breastfeeding Blues—
Myths About Breastfeeding

New moms often get "the blues" when they run up against the reality of life with a baby, as Deborah relates in her story. She talks about surprise after surprise, showing again how difficult it is to really *know* what the pregnancy, birth and parenting process will be like. You can no more truly know what becoming a parent is like by talking to other parents, than you can know what Hawaii is like by looking at travel brochures and posters. You can prepare yourself to a certain extent, but your experience will be uniquely yours, and slightly different from every other mother you know.

Deborah felt like a failure as a mom as she struggled with the difficulties of initial breastfeeding. Her feelings of failure can be traced fairly directly to the powerful cultural myth of the mothering instinct. Shirley battled the same myth in her story. In this myth, new mothers are told, "Just relax—you will know what to do" or "Breastfeeding is natural—of course you can do it."

These myths imply that every woman should be able to breeze through these new tasks and roles—being a mother, breastfeeding one's baby—just because she is a woman. By implication, if these roles and tasks are natural, women often assume that if they have trouble with them then they must be lacking in some natural ability. With that kind of reasoning running through your head, feeling like a failure is inevitable.

Pain and Breastfeeding

Deborah illustrates an aspect of the postpartum experience that many women are unprepared for: pain. She had much more pain as she tried to adjust to breastfeeding than she thought she would. While many women feel discomfort with nursing as their nipples toughen up, for a small percentage of women the sensation is much more than discomfort—it is actual pain. According to Jeannette Crenshaw, IBCLC, a certified lactation consultant and Family Education Coordinator at Presbyterian Hospital of Dallas, most new mothers have normal breast discomfort for about thirty to sixty seconds when they first start a feeding. This tenderness subsides as the baby swallows more, and usually peaks between day three and day five. This pain markedly improves as the milk supply increases and should be gone completely in seven to ten days.

If a nursing mother has pain that lasts the whole feeding or continues past ten days, she certainly needs to consult a lactation specialist. Pain such as this often indicates the baby is not latching on correctly or is positioned in an awkward way. It is admirable that Deborah, and others who feel this extended discomfort, can persist with the breastfeeding.

Please do not get the idea that breastfeeding is extremely difficult, or complicated, or always painful. According to Judy Eastburn, IBCLC, a certified breastfeeding consultant in Dallas, Texas, breastfeeding is on the same continuum as getting pregnant and giving birth to a baby. Getting pregnant is pretty easy most of the time—remember how easy it seemed when you were a teen, especially if you listened to the warnings of your health teacher? But some couples need a bit of medical intervention to accomplish this goal—fertility treatments, medications, in-vitro labs.

Likewise, giving birth is a natural and easy process—consider the stories of women in cultures where it is customary to just squat in the fields. A certain percentage of women, however, require medical intervention such as C-sections, pitocin drips or labor induction. Breastfeeding is simply a natural extension of this continuum. For some women, the baby latches right on, soreness is minimal, milk is plentiful. For others, the learning curve may be a bit greater, and the new mother may need the input of a qualified lactation consultant as well as a bit more time to make adjustments.

Deborah's experience is a great example of this. She persisted, got a little extra input and sailed on to a satisfying conclusion. Judy Eastburn tells us that difficulties latching on, as Deborah and Leila had, occur in maybe as many as 30 percent of those new moms who have some trouble with breastfeeding. In other words, difficulties with breastfeeding are not at all rare. They do not mean that a mom is a failure.

Postpartum Pain

Deborah also experienced pain related to her surgery—giving birth by cesarean section. Certainly most women, as they approach their baby's birth, mentally prepare themselves for labor pain. That is a given. Yet another myth comes into play with regard to pain for many pregnant women. They often think, *After the birth, I am home free physically. I will be done with backaches and swollen ankles.* Few women realize that pain is often a large part of postpartum recovery. I can remember complaining to the OB/GYN after the birth of my first baby because my back muscles felt sore, as if I had been moving pianos all weekend. He explained to me that I had used those muscles to the fullest during the pushing phase, so of course I was a little sore.

Episiotomy pain is another surprise to many women, as is hemorrhoid pain. In fact, researchers Anne Woollett and Mel Parr found that new mothers they interviewed perceived the slow process of physical recovery as one of the hardest postpartum adjustments.

This discussion of pain is not intended to scare an expectant mother, but rather to present an accurate picture of what the experience may be like. When you have an idea of what you might be feeling, you can better plan ways to take care of yourself physically. For coping with postpartum pain, follow these strategies:

- Take credit for what your body has been through. Even though birth is a normal process, all that pushing and pulling and stretching takes a toll on your body.
- Follow the recommendations of your healthcare professional regarding pain medication, sitz baths and activity levels.
- Give yourself time for pampering and physical recovery.

Persistence in the Face of Myth

As was discussed in Sarah's story in chapter 3, persistence in the face of difficulty learning a new job or skill is important. You didn't learn to ride a bike on the first attempt. You had to fall down, skin your knee, scrape your shins on the pedals and get blisters on your hands from gripping the handles too tightly. But you hung in there—you knew that learning something new usually requires perseverance. Because of the myth that being a mother or breastfeeding is easy, instinctual or natural, a woman may feel she is flawed, defective or a failure if it doesn't feel easy to her at first. Deborah showed great determination, listening to rational support from her mother and sister. Just as Shirley did in chapter 1, Deborah paid attention to reason: "Babies cry" and "Everything will be all right."

A Trick for Tunnel Vision

If, like Deborah, you can only see the endlessness of sleepless nights and being chained to the couch feeding the baby, try this strategy:

Get yourself a month-by-month calendar, the kind with 1.5 inch squares for each day, and a pack of highlighter-type markers. Then keep it handy and color-code each day.

Was today a good day with some triumphs and new skills learned (by you or baby)? Outline the day in pink.

Was today a "bad" day, full of tears and frustrations? Maybe the blue marker suits your mood best, so outline the day in blue.

Neutral days can be yellow.

Take a moment to record your reactions to each day in this manner. You will be able to see at a glance that the pink days are increasing, a sure sign that this difficult time is really passing. On the other hand, if the blue days are increasing, please see the section on postpartum stresses at the end of this book.

Most of the time, this relaxed attitude is difficult, but it has a great payoff in making the new mom feel better. Deborah reined in her worries and hung in there. She and her baby both benefited from a wonderful breastfeeding relationship.

Just as in learning anything new, the more you hang in there and really immerse yourself in the whole process, the easier it gets. Deborah was putting all her energy into figuring out the mother role, her baby and breastfeeding in particular. Focused only on that, she felt chained to the couch—because that was the center of all her efforts and energy. It was her life—for weeks. When all your energy and focus is on one particular aspect of your life in this way, it is difficult to see past the present moment. Breastfeeding and sitting on that couch may seem as if they are all you will ever do. It is a challenge to look ahead to different times when you haven't arrived there yet—especially when all your psychic energy is focused on the task of the moment.

Immersion in the culture of having an infant is easier when you have friends, sisters, moms who understand it. Deborah tells us that, too. It helps to know other mothers who have been through this dim tunnel and come out the other side. It helps to know you are not the only one who has found this adjustment to a new baby to be hard. Such knowledge helps debunk the myth that "there is something wrong with me." If your best friend or aunt had a similar experience, it must not be you who is the problem.

Struggling with the new task of mothering is simply a universal part of the process, not a flaw in you. It helps to know that you are not alone. Research has shown that women who have partners or sisters or friends who encourage them in breastfeeding are more likely to succeed at the task. Likewise, women who have other women to talk to who are in the same boat—parents of infants and toddlers—feel less depression after the birth of a baby.

As you embark on the journey into motherhood, prepare yourself well by connecting with other women. Talk openly with women you know who are parents already. Build your network of support through childbirth education classes, breastfeeding classes, support groups, parent education groups or your religious organization. You can strengthen your skills as a parent, boost your mood, have fun and make lifelong friendships by making it a priority to spend time with other parents of small children.

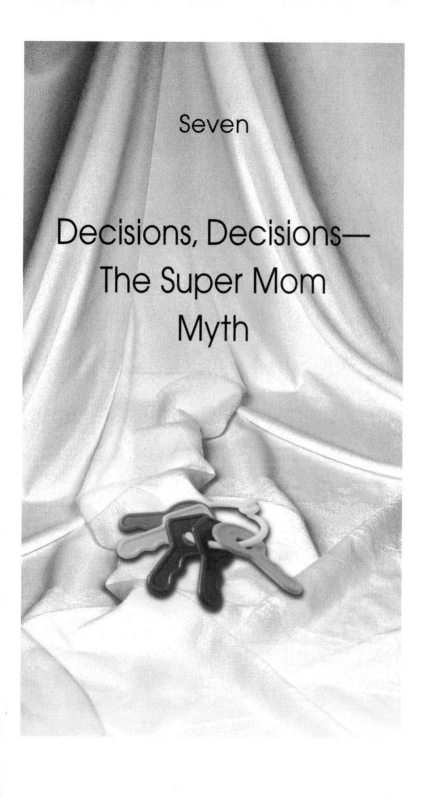

Seven

Decisions, Decisions— The Super Mom Myth

Super Mom—
Myth or Reality?

The title of "super mom" is bandied about these days, sometimes tongue in cheek and sometimes as a compliment. Super mom is omnipotent, all-knowing and perfect in every way, from her own physical appearance and her child's coordinated outfit to her spotless home. She never makes mistakes and her children are always smart, happy and well-behaved. The rest of us are mere mortals with spit-up on our shirts, dust bunnies in the hall and children who throw tantrums in the supermarket checkout line. Let yourself off the hook—super mom is a myth. The reality is we are all human.

My name is Kimberly Washington.
I am an accountant and the proud mother
of a beautiful little girl.

Baby's Name: _Kelsey LeeAnne_

Date of Birth: _August 7, 1999_

Time of Birth: _9:46 P.M._

Weight: _7 pounds, 9 ounces_

Length: _20 ½ inches_

When Kelsey was born I felt like sunshine on a bright new day. I was excited, thrilled, overjoyed and, I must admit, a little nervous—especially when my doctor placed her in my arms the first time. I was happy to see my baby and happy to know she was healthy. I thought I would cry tears of joy when I first saw Kelsey, but I didn't. Those didn't come until a couple of hours later when the fact that I was a mother started to embrace me. Then it seemed as if I cried all the time. I was elated to have a wonderful baby and to be a new mother.

The day we left the hospital started out great. I was exhilarated because I was taking Kelsey home. My husband drove our car to the front of the hospital, opened the back passenger side door and carefully strapped Kelsey into her infant car seat. I quickly climbed in the back and buckled up in the seat next to her. As we headed home I couldn't take my eyes off Kelsey. She looked so sweet and so tiny. Then *bam!* Out of the blue, I started crying uncontrollably. To this day, I don't know why I cried, but I did.

> *. . . I couldn't take my eyes off Kelsey. She looked so sweet and so tiny. . . . Out of the blue I started crying uncontrollably.*
>
> —KIMBERLY WASHINGTON

I figured my emotions were stirred by the enormous sense of responsibility I suddenly felt. I was determined to be a good mother. I remember thinking to myself, *This is it. You have to do or die.* Knowing the fate of my precious little baby girl was in my hands played heavily on my mind. While I considered myself to be a competent, responsible adult, I questioned whether I could properly take care of Kelsey. Knowing I was responsible for another life hit me like a ton of bricks, and that reality consumed my every thought. I had only been responsible for me before. Now I had a baby who was totally dependent on me to take care of her, protect her and make decisions for her. I wasn't sure if I was ready for such a challenging task.

I felt comfortable providing basic care for my baby—bathing her, feeding her and changing her—but I wasn't really prepared for many other things involved in mothering. For example, it took me a while to learn what my baby's different cries meant—that is, whether she was hungry, wet or wanted to be held. Not knowing those kinds of things was incredibly frustrating, and I felt guilty for not having the knowledge. I was also incredibly worried about making important decisions for my baby, especially involving her health.

One day when Kelsey was about three months old I noticed she was having problems digesting formula. I took her to see her pediatrician, but she was off for the day. One of her colleagues treated Kelsey, and after thoroughly examining her, prescribed two different medications. While I was relieved he had diagnosed what was wrong with Kelsey, I was concerned about her having to take so much medication. It really bothered me.

A couple of days later I called Kelsey's regular pediatrician and shared my concerns. She suggested I bring my baby to her office for an examination. After a thorough checkup, the doctor recommended I stop giving Kelsey one of the medications and shorten the time she had to take the other one. I carefully considered her advice and decided to follow it to the letter. Then I wondered whether I had made the right choice. Struggling, I weighed the two doctors' recommendations again and decided to stick with my decision to cut back on the medication.

What if I didn't make the right decision? I thought. I could not live with myself if Kelsey's condition got worse because of a choice I made. I watched her like a hawk for the next few days and checked on her over and over to see how she reacted to the change in medication. Fortunately, Kelsey recovered from her ailment quickly and didn't have any negative side effects. It wasn't long before she was back to her old self again.

I have a lot of respect for doctors, but as a mother I have to make the final decision about what treatment is best for my baby. That is an awesome responsibility. Even now, when I have to make decisions for Kelsey, whether simple or complicated ones, I find myself analyzing the situation over and over again. And if need be, I investigate and research the problem as if preparing for a college term paper. I make sure I have as much information as possible before I decide what to do. Then I make a decision and pray I made the right choice.

Kimberly's Savvy Strategies

- When faced with big decisions, check in with those who know you best: your doctor, a trusted partner or a friend.

- Take a deep breath and trust *yourself* once you make a decision.

Kimberly struggled with making decisions about her baby's welfare. Most new mothers do. Analysis of her situation will be presented after Angela's story. Angela faced a dilemma with her baby that was similar to Kimberly's.

My name is Angela Hsu.
I am a commercial real estate attorney
and the proud mother of a
beautiful little girl.

Baby's Name: *Julia Celine*

Date of Birth: *December 16, 2000*

Time of Birth: *5:03 P.M.*

Weight: *7 pounds, 9 ounces*

Length: *20 inches*

I was overwhelmed when I first saw my baby. Everything about her was amazing to me. I could not believe she was so perfect and complete, with all of her fingers and toes. That reality blew my mind. Because of the sophistication of medical technology I knew early on that my little girl appeared to be developing nicely without any complications. The reality of her perfect little body, however, was still astounding.

It's hard for me to articulate how I felt immediately after I delivered Julia. Joy comes to mind, but I felt so much more than that. It was an exhilarating experience—one that was extremely intimate and personal. I spent hours holding my baby and marveling at her perfectly smooth, round face. I know it sounds clichéd, but I believe you have to experience giving life to really know what it feels like.

While I was fascinated by my baby's development, it also scared me.

—ANGELA HSU

I knew I was a mother on an intellectual level, but the full sense of the word and the responsibilities that go along with it didn't hit me until my daughter was about six months old. Before that, she was this cute, little, adorable plaything I enjoyed caring for and interacting with. When Julia's personality and identity began to emerge, however, she was a unique person, not just someone for whom I had to provide basic care.

That was a profound realization for me. By watching my baby—the way she observed things, what made her smile, how she dealt with frustration—I was able to get a glimpse of what she was going to be like as she grew older. Julia had grown beyond reflexive and instinctive reactions. She was thinking for, and clearly expressing, herself: *I'm hungry. I'm sleepy. I want my favorite toy.* While I was fascinated by my baby's development, it also scared me.

I felt uneasy because I didn't want to make any wrong decisions or mistakes that might negatively affect my child's personality. I had read so much confusing and conflicting literature about how sensitive babies are, and how parents influence their children's behavior. The overwhelming amount of information available led me to question whether *anyone* knew the right thing to do.

For example, the walls in my baby's room are stacked with toys, books and clothes. She is the youngest of two grandchildren on my side of the family and the only grandchild on my husband's side of the family. Because of this my baby is constantly lavished with gifts and attention.

Like most parents, I don't want to raise a spoiled child. But on the other hand, as a mother, I want my baby to have everything—including all the love in the world. I couldn't help wondering, however, whether she was getting too much? Looking back on my own childhood, I was reminded that my mother made most of my clothes and toys. While we were far from poor, I did not have a lot of material things, and I worked hard to acquire the possessions I did have. I started working in my parent's thirty-unit motel in Los Angeles when I was nine years old. I did everything from operating a switchboard to cleaning rooms. My parents were frugal, but I always felt their abundant love and never questioned it.

My husband, a doctor, was brought up the same way. He also started working when he was very young: flipping burgers, scooping ice cream and frying chicken. Having to work for material things instilled good values in us and gave us a strong sense of humility toward others, a respect for hard work and a solid code of ethics. While pretty clothes and fun toys are fine, a great sense of values is what I want for my baby.

I believe strong morals, values and ethics are key to the development of my baby's personality. As Julia grows up, I want her to understand and appreciate the value of chores and responsibilities. I don't want her to expect everything to be handed to her on a silver platter, and I don't want her to think that she is somehow better than people who are less fortunate.

Sometimes, when I look at my daughter, I can tell the little wheels that turn her thoughts are spinning. I wonder what she is thinking. Will I be able to create a good environment that fosters her emotional development? When she smiles or coos at me, I know Julia is depending on me to help her grow and develop into a wonderful human being with a pleasing personality. Through her eyes, I am discovering the world all over again. Through this great adventure of mothering, I'm determined to help my baby be the best person she can be.

Angela's Savvy Strategies

- Study your baby to learn what she is saying about her preferences.

- Examine your own values regularly, and keep your parenting in line with those values.

Decisions, Decisions:
Facing the Myth of "Super Mom"

Parents have a great responsibility raising their babies to adulthood. There are big decisions and small decisions all along the way. Mothers and fathers are often judged on their parenting abilities, even their value as people, based on the outcome of their parenting efforts. What kind of kid will your child turn out to be? What can you do to raise a "good kid," one you can be proud of? Kimberly and Angela are very tuned into these questions. The weight of this responsibility was the focus of each woman's transition to parenthood. Jane Weaver and Jane Ussher also found this to be true in their sample of first-time moms. Most of the women they interviewed were in awe of this obligation from the moment they first held their babies.

Good Mom, Bad Mom

Parents can live up to this assignment to produce upstanding young citizens if they keep their expectations in perspective. New parents often feel this responsibility is overwhelming because of how society views parents: as either good or bad. There is no middle ground. New parents, in particular, are sucked into this either/or thinking. *If I can respond to my baby with patience, recognize his needs, stop his crying and get him to sleep, then I am a good mother. If I cannot do all these things, I am a bad mother.*

Kimberly was afraid she would be a bad mother for trusting the opinion of one doctor over the other. Angela feared being a bad mother by producing a spoiled child, one with many toys and pretty clothes. Sarah felt like a bad mother because she could not get her twin girls to fall asleep. Shirley felt like a bad mother for not knowing how to suction her son's nose with that strange bulb syringe. Even while putting these demands on themselves as mothers, most women know deep inside that it is clearly impossible to be a good mother *all the time.*

Psychologists Stephanie Brown, Rhonda Small and Judith Lumley asked ninety new mothers what it meant to be a good mother. They compared the responses of women who had experienced postpartum depression with the responses of women who had no history of depression. Both groups universally agreed that good mothers are patient, understanding, loving, caring and attentive. Good mothers spend quality time with their children, get to know their children and their needs and guide them according to those needs. Just as all the new mothers could agree on these criteria, they all also admitted the criteria were impossible to match all the time. They knew they were buying into the super mom myth, and that it was impossible to "live" that myth. Still, they kept trying to do just that.

Talking to Yourself About Super Mom

New mothers, take heed. Consider that being a good mother is not a dichotomy of good versus bad, where you either succeed or you fail. Accomplishment in parenting is quite relative. All parents make mistakes. If you are lucky and work hard, the good things, the times when you do well, will outweigh the times when you are cranky, irritable, fatigued or too busy for your children. Give yourself room to be a human kind of parent, rather than a super mom. You will never succeed in living that myth—no one does. Perfect is just a concept—not an actuality.

The pressure to be a super mom is compounded by a culture that tends to blame mothers for their children's behavior. The blaming can be subtle: smiling at a mom with a well-behaved child in the grocery store, while scowling at a mother whose child is screaming. The blaming can also be

A Quick Guide to Instilling Good Values

If you want your child to . . .	Follow these guidelines . . .
Feel loved	Be affectionate and say "I love you" often
Love reading	Read to your child every day
Be curious	Ask your child questions and answer his patiently
Be confident	Provide your child opportunities to succeed and to fail
Be assertive	Allow your child to debate with you and respect his view
Be physically fit	Engage in physical activities as a family and as an individual
Be generous	Demonstrate charity

more direct—for example, when psychologists explore the background of a criminal and focus on his relationship with his mother.

Kimberly and Angela seemed to feel that they were alone in experiencing the pressure of making decisions for their babies. The reality is that fathers are just as important to how a child turns out, whether that father is present or not. An absent father definitely influences how a child grows to adulthood. Extended family, religious institutions, educational institutions, family friends and same-age peers are also powerful in shaping the child into an adult. It is not a simple formula of "mom + kid = adult." Mothers need not feel all the weight on their shoulders alone; nor should they exaggerate their individual importance in how a child grows into an adult.

Developmental theorists and psychologists have long argued over the relative importance of family and environment (the influence of nurturing) versus genetic influences (the influence of nature) in how children turn out. The "nature" side asserts that children will be what they will be— without much influence from parents. The "nurture" view gives much power to the parents' influence on their child. If Kimberly and Angela believed that their actions would not make much difference in what sort of people Kelsey and Julia were as adults, they would be much less worried. The bottom line is that nature and nurture are both important. All human beings are a complex mix of both.

The Myth of Control

The control myth appears again in this debate in yet another variation. Can parents actually control what kind of adults their children become? Certainly parents can guide a child in a specific direction by deciding what values they want to teach that child and making parenting decisions accordingly. Consider writing a "mission statement." Sit down with your partner and discuss what you want your child to be as an adult. Do you want your child to feel loved—and to be loving? Have a questioning mind? Be able to defend himself?

Decide which qualities and values are most important to instill in your child. Write them down, and use them to guide your interactions with your child from day one. If you want your child to feel loved and to be loving, be affectionate with him and tell him he is loved. If you want your child to be intelligent and literate, read to him. If you want your child to be charitable and giving, demonstrate those qualities in your own behavior and engage her in exercises in giving as soon as she is able. Do you want your child to be confident and outspoken? Listen to her, support her ability to form her own opinions and respect those opinions—even if it means offering a choice between green beans and beets when you would rather cook only one vegetable!

When you have identified the values that you wish to instill in your child and are modeling those values on a regular basis, the next step is to trust yourself. Know that you can be a "good enough" parent. Do not chastise yourself, for example, for not knowing all the baby's cries, as Kimberly did. If some issue stumps you, get more information. If two doctors offer different treatments, research the choices or get a third opinion. Sometimes a structured decision-making format, like that outlined below, can be helpful.

Decision-Making Steps

1. Define the problem.
2. Gather information from diverse sources: books, other parents, health-care professionals.
3. Weigh the importance of the facts you have gathered in several ways:
   - Divide them into "pros" and "cons."
   - Talk them through with your partner or trusted family or friends.
   - Think logically and group the facts based on your values and preferences.
4. Pick a course of action and stick to it for a brief trial period. Know that you can try it for awhile, collect information about how it is working and change course if you're not happy with the first outcome.
5. Trust that you made the best decision you could for now, given the facts you have.

While this structured plan works for some parents, others prefer a more intuitive style. You may just want to go with your gut instinct. Other parents find that their faith is a significant support when faced with decisions. Exercise your faith, put your trust in God, pray and listen for an answer. Rely on your religious leadership for guidance or support in your prayers if needed.

Aiming for "Good Enough" Parenting

If you make a decision and it crashes and burns, remember that parenting is not a "bad apple" proposition. One bad decision or less-than-positive outcome will not "ruin" the whole barrel, that is, your developing child. Don't exaggerate your error. Instead, try to follow these principles:

- Forgive yourself.
- Determine how to make better choices the next time the situation arises.
- Remember that children are resilient, and the good parenting will outweigh the "bad" over time.
- Trust in yourself over the long run.
- Give yourself a pat on the back for controlling what you can in your child's life.

If you find that you are not able to be the parent you want to be, that you are often cranky or overwhelmed or not thinking clearly, it may be that you need to take more time for yourself. It is easier to be patient, caring and attentive to your child when you are rested and have had a break, than it is when you are tired and running on empty. Taking care of you is one of the best ways to ensure that you are being the best parent that you can be.

Eight

Family Foundation—
The Family Ties
Myths

Family Ties—Myths or Reality?

Family Ties Myth Number 1: Your relationship with your first family will not change when you become a parent. This is a variation on the "hidden" myth addressed in chapter 2, that is, that your life will remain unchanged after childbirth. You may believe becoming a parent will not affect your place in your family of origin. Just as your marriage and your view of self inevitably are altered by this new baby, so will your relationship with your first family need revision.

Family Ties Myth Number 2: You need supportive family and/or a positive family model to be a good parent. Common sense says that if you had parents who were good parental role models, you may find it easier to parent your own child in a positive way. But having a positive family example is not necessary for you to be a good parent. You can learn skills from multiple sources, and if you had a less than ideal family background, you can still be a good parent.

My name is María Baquero.
I am a stay-at-home mom and vice-chair
of the National Society of Hispanic MBAs.
I am also the proud mother of
a beautiful little girl.

Baby's Name: _María Elena_

Date of Birth: _July 24, 2000_

Time of Birth: _2:06 A.M._

Weight: _6 pounds, 3 ounces_

Length: _18½ inches_

I grew up in a close-knit family in Bayamón, Puerto Rico. My parents taught my four siblings and me to love, honor and respect family. They also encouraged us to support one another and be there for each other no matter what. After I graduated from high school, I moved to Massachusetts to attend Boston University. That's where I met my husband, Angel.

Six months after my husband and I moved from Chicago to Scottsdale, Arizona, I discovered I was pregnant. Angel and I were very

After my family arrived, I sometimes felt overwhelmed— like I didn't have a minute to myself.

—María Baquero

excited. However, because I had an ectopic pregnancy a few months earlier, we welcomed the news with guarded optimism. We told our families I was expecting, and everyone was excited—especially my sister Elena. She and I are very close.

About a month later, Elena called and told me she was also pregnant. I was thrilled for her and loved the idea of going through our pregnancies together. Because Elena was already a mother I depended on her to help guide me along and tell me what to expect on our magnificent journey. It could not have been a better time for us. Our babies were growing and developing without incident. I was exercising, eating right and getting excellent prenatal care. Everything was perfect.

In my sixth month, however, I received devastating news: Elena lost her baby. I was heartbroken for her, and I began to worry about the safety of my baby. I thought because my sister and I had gone through the whole emotion of passing the three-month period that we were home free and would not encounter any problems. I was wrong.

During my next scheduled appointment with my doctor I requested another ultrasound to make sure my baby was all right. Curious, she asked why I felt so strongly about it. After I explained what happened to my sister my doctor agreed another ultrasound was warranted. Without hesitating, she thoroughly examined my baby again. I was relieved to know she was healthy and developing nicely.

Amid the pain and sadness surrounding my sister's loss, I tried to be strong and prepare for my baby's arrival. My husband and I moved into a bigger house. My mother came to visit from Puerto Rico and helped us get settled. She also helped lift my spirits, kept me focused and was with me when my beautiful baby girl was born. My daughter was so tiny and as cute as could be. She also had a head full of black hair, just like her daddy. In honor of my sister, I named my daughter María Elena. When I shared the news with my sister she cried tears of joy.

Our stay in the hospital was not without incident. My husband and I had a little scare when María Elena stopped breathing during her initial checkup in the nursery. She was taken to the neonatal intensive care unit (NICU). I was stricken with fear. When I was finally allowed to visit my baby I was not prepared for what I saw. My little María Elena was hooked up to several tubes and monitors. I could not handle seeing her that way. I had been so excited when María Elena was born. In my mind she was perfect. It was hard for me to accept something was wrong with her, and I didn't know how to handle the myriad of emotions that enveloped me.

Several doctors examined María Elena thoroughly. After a battery of tests they discovered some of the pain medication I was given during labor had gotten into her system. Fortunately, she recovered and was released from the NICU a day later. I was grateful and relieved my baby received a clean bill of health.

That wonderful news fueled my desire to take María Elena home. I was ready to go, and I couldn't wait for my baby to meet the rest of our family. I was so proud of her. However, the day my in-laws and my father were to arrive from Puerto Rico, I had a long crying spell. Try as I might, I could not hold back the tears. My husband, a wonderfully patient man, tried unsuccessfully to help me figure out the source of my sadness. I knew my father and my in-laws were coming. I had known for months. We had planned for their visit, but I just wasn't ready for more company.

Don't misunderstand me—I love my family. I was excited that they were coming to meet my precious little girl. In retrospect, however, I didn't feel like I had enough time to settle down as a new family—just my husband, María Elena and me—without a lot of people around. All the commotion was too much. I couldn't bear it. After my family arrived, I sometimes felt overwhelmed—like I didn't have a minute to myself.

There were days when I felt there were just too many people in the house, and I needed to get away—escape. I would take María Elena to my room and lock the door. We would stay there for hours because I didn't want to talk to anybody. Then a huge wave of guilt would wash over me, causing me tremendous pain. I love my family, and I knew they wanted to help us and share our joy. But I could not bring myself out of the dark mood that swallowed me. I kept thinking, *I am a successful businessperson who is used to thinking rationally, taking the emotions out of situations and moving on in order to achieve the best results.* But no matter how hard I tried, I could not snap out of my dismal mood.

Figuring out exactly what I needed was another challenge. One minute I wanted to be alone and the next minute I wanted company. One morning, my parents, in-laws and my husband went out and I stayed home with María Elena. I was thrilled just thinking about the two of us being alone together and bonding. When they all left, however, I wanted them to come back. I was going from one extreme to the other, my emotions swinging like a pendulum.

Things finally started to settle down after my family went back to Puerto Rico, and my husband and I got into a routine with María Elena. Yes, my emotions still come and go a bit, but for the most part I am on an even keel. And as I continue to enjoy María Elena and juggle visits from relatives, I have a deeper appreciation for family. After all, there is nothing more important.

María's Savvy Strategies

- Balance time between your new family—your partner and baby—and your extended family and friends.
- Talk supportively to yourself when feelings rage, reminding yourself of pre-existing strengths and skills.

Analysis of María's experience with her extended family is discussed in depth after Marielle's story.

My name is Marielle Arrieh Johary.
I am a radiologist and the proud mother
of a beautiful little boy.

Baby's Name: _A. J. (Albert, Jr.)_

Date of Birth: _January 11, 2000_

Time of Birth: _7:59 P.M._

Weight: _9 pounds, 1 ounce_

Length: _21½ inches_

I miss my parents. I didn't realize how much until I gave birth to my son, A. J. My mom passed away in 1995; my father four years later. I was hoping and praying my dad would live long enough to meet my beautiful baby. I made arrangements for him to spend Thanksgiving and Christmas with my family, and be with me when A. J. was born, but that didn't happen. My father succumbed to kidney failure a couple of months before my baby arrived. It was an incredibly painful time for me. However, cherishing loving memories of my parents helped ease my pain.

I remember when I was pregnant and how frequently I flew back and forth from Atlanta to Dallas to visit my father.

I felt my parents' presence. It was so strong, I could practically see them standing on either side of my bed.

—MARIELLE ARRIEH JOHARY

While it was stressful, I am thankful for the time I spent with him. Some days my dad and I would sit and have long philosophical conversations that lasted for hours. We talked about everything under the sun, especially my pregnancy. Excited, I told my father about my ultrasound and showed him the grainy black and white pictures of my adorable baby.

Staring at my son's image, my father beamed with pride. Then, as if deep in thought, he proceeded to give me advice to pass along to his grandson. I can still hear my father's voice when he shared his thoughts on family. He told me, "Parents are your best friends and will remain so all of your life. Your children are your dearest possessions, and you must work hard to build their character. And parents should never, never divorce." In our Middle Eastern culture, my father explained, "You stick it out no matter what."

When I think about that moment, and others, a huge smile covers my face. My dad was a wonderful man. He was very serious and conservative. A graduate of Harvard law school, he spent his life working as a corporate attorney. Shortly after that visit, my dad died. I was deeply saddened. I had lost both my parents. A strong sense of loneliness embraced me: Neither of them would be with me during a very special time in my life.

After careful consideration, my doctor decided to induce labor because my baby was a week late. At one point, he thought I was going to need a C-section. After consulting with my husband Al and me, my physician left the room. My husband followed to change into scrubs. As I sat in bed alone in the room I began to worry about the procedure and whether my baby was going to be okay. That was my main concern.

My thoughts were suddenly interrupted by an overwhelming sense of my parents' presence. It was so strong, I could practically see them standing on either side of my bed. Then I felt a calming peace wash over me. A few minutes later, my husband and doctor returned to the delivery room. After a thorough examination, my physician informed us that I no longer needed a C-section.

It was as if my parents had given me an inner peace that

helped me relax and progress through my labor. I was over-joyed. After my baby was born, a nurse cleaned him up and brought him to me. When my eyes rested on A. J., I started crying and couldn't stop. It was the most beautiful moment. He looked like my father and reminded me so much of him. A. J. also had facial expressions and hand gestures like my dad. I was deeply moved every time he put his little index fin-ger up to his mouth as if he was deep in thought—just like Dad. At that moment, I felt like my parents were still with me sharing my joy.

When I held A. J. in my arms the first time, I felt like I had become my mother. I was doing things the way she would have. That night, a nurse wanted to take my baby to the nurs-ery so that I could rest, but I couldn't let him go. I wanted my son with me all the time. I remember when I was a child how protective my mother was of me and my sisters. We were her focus in life. Everything she did was for us. I felt the same way about my son. I was genuinely moved by how receptive the nurse was to my wishes. She gave me my baby without question, and he stayed with me the whole time I was in the hospital.

Even when we went home, I couldn't get enough of A. J. I checked on him all the time, especially when he was sleeping to make sure he was breathing. I must have looked in on him a million times. I was on a serious adrenaline rush. I couldn't rest no matter how hard I tried. My husband couldn't believe the energy I had. I felt like super mom—not only able to leap tall buildings, but lift them, too. However, after a few weeks,

I totally crashed. I lost all of my energy. I was exhausted, and I suffered short-term memory loss. Forgetting little things became a big problem. I remember calling my girlfriend on more than one occasion and forgetting why I had called.

Crying spells were another problem. I had them frequently. One day, A. J. was colicky and wouldn't stop crying. Out of the blue, I started crying, too—perhaps because I couldn't comfort him. By this time, my mother-in-law who had come to visit had left, my husband had gone back to work and I was home alone with A. J. I worried constantly about whether I was caring for him properly. With hindsight, today I know I was, but at that time it was all I thought about. I went about my days entirely focused on A. J. He was always on my mind, even when I went to bed at night. It was the strangest thing.

I soon learned, however, to take mothering one day at a time, and it's proved very helpful. I finally started to feel like my old self again after A. J. started sleeping through the night—which allowed me to sleep, too. He was about four and half months old when that happened.

During my down time, I did a lot of thinking and soul searching. Along the way, I discovered how important my baby is to me. A. J. is my top priority. It seems strange now when I reflect on how career-focused I was before he was born. I worked extremely hard all the time. I invested thirteen years' training in my career as a radiologist. I did a fellowship after my residency and made full partner after three years with my practice. I was gung ho about my career. I had been that way about medicine ever since I was four years old, going around with my little black medical bag looking for hurt animals to mend.

However, after A. J. was born, everything changed. While my career is still important to me, it's secondary. My family and my friends are most important. And I make a concerted effort to develop our relationships even more. Being a good mother to A. J. and being home with him is also very important to me. I remember as though it were yesterday, how happy I was when I came home from school and my mom was there—greeting me with open arms and asking about my day.

That's one reason I decided to work out of my home. I wanted to spend as much time as possible with A. J., so I had an extra room in my home converted into an office complete with the tools necessary to perform my job: view boxes to read X rays, a fax machine and a telephone. An outpatient radiology imaging center delivers X rays to my husband, an internist. He brings them home from his office, and I read them. Dictating reports to a medical transcriptionist at the imaging center is the final step in the process. I complete that task over the telephone.

I love working in this fashion because it allows me to accomplish my goal of spending more time with A. J. My parents were so involved in my life and the lives of my sisters. They were very concerned about us and always there, always caring, always lavishing us with love. My mom and dad were good, decent people and the absolute best role models. I didn't have to look beyond our home to find my heroes. They were always there.

When I reflect on my life, I can't remember a time when my parents disappointed me. They were the best. I loved them so much, and I thank God for them. While my mom and dad are gone they will never be forgotten. And my son will know them because they are a part of me—and of him.

Marielle's Savvy Strategies

- If your parents are no longer living, or are living across the country, trust that you can have their positive influence with you at all times by remembering what they have taught you about life and parenting.

- Be open to change in your life after your baby is born; you never can predict how your life may be transformed, just as Marielle changed her view of her career.

Family Foundation

María and Marielle launched into parenting with one of the best assets a parent can have—a firm foundation of supportive, close family relationships. New parents' most ready source of information about how to be a parent is the example of their own parents: mother and father. María and Marielle were each blessed with a background brimming with positive family values of closeness and affection.

Marielle illustrates this quite forthrightly when she says she was becoming her mother with A. J., acting as her mother would have with a new baby. She had a positive role model of putting baby first, sacrificing and loving for the baby's development. Her father had voiced these principles before his death saying, "Children are your dearest possessions." While new parents have many sources of information on how to be a parent, the most accessible model is their own parents. In times of stress, like having a baby, the natural instinct is to revert to how we were treated as children. How lucky for Marielle and María that their earliest models were full of love and closeness.

Balancing Loyalties to Family New and Old

This strong family foundation felt like a contradiction inside María in those first postpartum weeks. Her family had instilled in her their values of "love, respect and honor family." But she felt smothered by her family when they visited after the birth of María Elena. It is because she had this sense of "family as a priority" that she wanted to be on her own, with just her husband and her baby.

When a couple marries, each leaves the families in which they were raised. They begin to put primary loyalty on their new family of two. When the couple has a baby, this focus on their new family is intensified. María was feeling torn between the family that raised her (her family of origin) and her new family. In that sense, she was simply carrying out the principles learned from her first family: She wanted to focus her energy on loving and building the relationship with her husband and their new baby.

This is a normal, natural part of the transition to becoming a family. The new mother vacillates between her two families, new and old. With time, as the bond in the new family strengthens, the new mom feels more relaxed. She can relinquish a bit of the tie to her family of origin. If the new family does not take time to connect, they are not honoring the family of origin's tradition of closeness.

It would have helped María to understand that her impulse to have time with just her husband and María Elena was actually the beginning of recreating that close-knit family for her daughter. María's advice to new parents on planning extended family visits is good. The help of extended family members is often invaluable when a new baby is born. But many couples prefer to have a week or more to themselves. They want to be by themselves as they figure out this new baby and their new roles. Once they feel more like a real family, grandparents or aunts or cousins can be invited to bond with the baby and help the new mother. If both parents cannot take parental leave, that transition may be more extended. Family help for the new mom may take precedence then.

Changing Family Ties

The stories of Marielle and María portray another inevitable facet in a new mother's life: Family relationships change. In chapter 2, the hidden myth that your life will remain the same after your baby is born was discussed. Thinking that your family relationships will stay constant is a simple variation on this myth. The foundation that one's first family provided is important, but taking on the new role of parent means reworking those old family relationships.

Family members may become closer—or more distant, as in María's feelings of connection to her family. You now relate to your family as an adult, an equal. It's time for you to sit at the grown-up table for holiday dinners—no more

Effective Family Help

In order to get the most from offers of help from family and friends, consider these ideas:

- Plan in advance and coordinate times for visits, so family members do not overlap and the help is spread out when you need it, rather than offered (and used up) all at once.
- List tasks for family members to do and assign specific chores to specific people. For example, put your mother-in-law in charge of meals and your father-in-law in charge of errands.
- Be direct about the fact that family members are there to assist, not to be entertained.

kids' table for you. The deep conversations Marielle shared with her father before he died are examples of this peer relationship. Her father treated her as an equal. She was worthy of serious conversations with him. He entrusted her with his wisdom about how families should be.

Because of this bond with her parents, and their role in her life as best friends, Marielle could feel their presence with her in spite of their deaths. Her closeness to them was deepened as she became a parent and shared that role with them. Looking at A. J., she could now understand fully how her own parents felt toward her and her sisters. Another way in which Marielle connected with her parents' values as she mothered A. J. was in her career priorities. She shifted her work commitments to second place, raising her relationship with her son to first. This was what her mother had demonstrated for her when she was a girl. In this way, she moved even more into line with her first family's values, reinforcing her feeling that she was like her mother.

Requirements for Good Enough Parenting

Having a strong family foundation like María and Marielle shared makes being a good enough parent easier. But it is a myth to think that you won't be a good parent if you lack the sort of firm background shared by Marielle and María. A loving, solid first family is not an absolute requirement for the job. In fact, most parents have at least one item on the list of "what I will do differently from my parents." Great parents exist who had terrible family backgrounds—filled with abuse, alcoholism, doubt and conflict. Take heart. If you lack a rosy family model, you can still be a good enough parent.

Learning to Be a Better Parent

Resources are plentiful to help parents override the effects of less-than-positive parenting when they were children. Consider these options:

- Look for parenting classes taught in religious institutions, school systems or mental health and hospital settings.
- Check out parenting books from your local library.
- Find parents whom you admire and study their relationships with their children. Good models are out there; just watch and learn.
- Effective parenting is even found in quality television and movies—sometimes.
- Consider counseling if educating yourself and trying new strategies just seems too hard without help.

Becoming a better parent is an admirable and achievable goal, no matter what your family background. Seek out the resources that fit for you and your learning style.

Grief and Loss in the Initiation Period

Marielle's adjustment to parenthood was complicated by her grief over the loss of her parents. Dealing with death while acquainting one's self with parenting increases the risk of postpartum depression. It demands facing emotions on many levels all at once. It is quite natural to feel heightened grief and loss when a baby is first born. Great sadness wells up at not having the deceased loved one able to see, hold and know this new baby.

As Marielle shows in her story, however, this grief subsides over time as the new parent realizes that the baby represents the continuity of life. A. J. reminded Marielle of her father, in looks and gestures. A. J. was his legacy. She knew, then, that memories of her father would stay with her, giving her a sense of his presence and love; and she would be able to convey stories about her father to her son, keeping her father alive in this sense. Grieving is often easier when the person who has experienced the loss finds ways to renew and continue the connection, rather than erasing the deceased from life and memories.

Strategies for Grieving

- Give yourself time and permission to feel the grief. Set aside "crying times" if needed, then switch gears to a pampering or fun activity to restore your focus on positive aspects of your life.
- Create a memorial for the lost person: plant a tree, fill a memory book.
- Practice a ritual of checking in with the deceased parent, such as meditating, talking with them in spirit or writing letters.

María's story was also touched by loss. Her sister lost the baby that she was carrying, and María had weathered an ectopic pregnancy. She reacted in an understandable way: She feared for the safety of her unborn baby. Pregnancy loss has that natural effect in the expectant mother. It may be difficult to trust that this baby will be all right until she can actually hold the baby in her arms. María's fears were increased because she and her sister thought they were out of the woods, past the time when most miscarriages occur. Having experienced a miscarriage with my second pregnancy, I confided my worries to my OB/GYN when pregnant with my second child. He reassured me, saying, "I don't imagine you will relax until this baby is a year old." And he was right.

The Perfect Baby Myth

María expressed feelings of loss about the perfect baby myth. New mothers universally expect that their babies will be perfect. Even if someone you know had a baby with a birth defect or illness, you have trouble believing it could happen to you. When she saw María Elena hooked up to all those tubes, it was upsetting. Not only was she worried about her baby, but it was difficult to accept that her baby was not perfect. The control myth is again at play here. María realized at that moment that she was not able to protect her child 100 percent.

Fortunately for María, her daughter's troubles were limited. Many new parents have to face a much more severe violation of the perfect baby myth. Babies can have major medical problems. Babies can be the "wrong" sex. Babies can remind new mothers of some family member they are alienated from and would rather forget. Babies can have difficult temperaments. There are lots of ways in which the baby that arrives is not what the new mom pictured.

One friend of mine really wanted a girl when she was expecting. She was from a family of many girls, and she was hesitant about her ability to understand and relate to a boy.

When she gave birth to her son, at first she was terrified. On the second day, she called me from the hospital and said, "You know what? He's just a baby. He's just a baby." Recognizing that fact, she was able to reassure herself. She would know what to do with him for many months and maybe years to come because he fell first into the category of baby, then into the category of boy.

When parents are faced with a baby who crashes their dreams, that is the lesson to remember. In spite of any discrepancy between what you expected and what arrived, your child is first and foremost a baby. Meet the baby's needs, and get to know your child for who she is. The rest will follow.

571567209

READER/CUSTOMER CARE SURVEY

We care about your opinions. Please take a moment to fill out this Reader Survey card and mail it back to us.
As a special **"thank you"**, we'll send you exciting news about interesting books and a valuable **Gift Certificate**

Please PRINT using ALL CAPITALS

BA3

First Name _____   Last Name _____   MI. ⊔

Address _____

City _____   ST ⊔⊔   Zip ⊔⊔⊔⊔⊔

Phone # (⊔⊔⊔) ⊔⊔⊔ - ⊔⊔⊔⊔   Fax # (⊔⊔⊔) ⊔⊔⊔ - ⊔⊔⊔⊔

Email _____

(1) Gender:
○ Female
○ Male

(2) Age:
○ 13-19   ○ 40-49
○ 20-29   ○ 50-59
○ 30-39   ○ 60+

(3) Your children's age(s):
Please fill in all that apply.
○ 6 or Under   ○ 15-18
○ 7-10   ○ 19+
○ 11-14

(8) Marital Status:
○ Married
○ Single
○ Divorced / Widowed

(9) Was this book:
○ Purchased For Yourself?
○ Received As a Gift?

(10) How many books in this series have you bought or read?
○ 1   ○ 3
○ 2   ○ 4+

(11) Did this book meet your expectations?
○ Yes
○ No

(12) How did you find out about this book? *Please fill in ONE.*
○ Personal Recommendation
○ Store Display
○ TV / Radio Program
○ Bestseller List
○ Website
○ Advertisement/Article or Book
○ Catalog or Mailing
○ Other _____

(13) What FIVE subject areas do you enjoy reading about most? *Rank only FIVE.*
Choose 1 for your favorite, 2 for second favorite, etc.

	1	2	3	4	5
Self Development	○	○	○	○	○
Parenting	○	○	○	○	○
Spirituality/Inspiration	○	○	○	○	○
Family and Relationships	○	○	○	○	○
Health and Nutrition	○	○	○	○	○
Recovery	○	○	○	○	○
Business/Professional	○	○	○	○	○
Entertainment	○	○	○	○	○
Sports	○	○	○	○	○
Teen Issues	○	○	○	○	○
Pets	○	○	○	○	○

6244567206

(18) Where do you purchase most of your books?
Please fill in your top TWO choices only.

○ General Bookstore
○ Religious Bookstore
○ Warehouse / Price Club
○ Discount or Other Retail Store
○ Website
○ Book Club / Mail Order

(20) What type(s) of magazines do you SUBSCRIBE to?
Fill in up to FIVE categories.

○ Parenting
○ Sports
○ Fashion
○ Business / Professional
○ World News / Current Events
○ General Entertainment
○ Homemaking, Cooking, Crafts
○ Women's Issues
○ Other (please specify) _____

(25) Are you:
○ A Parent?
○ A Grandparent

RED EYEGLASS SERIES

Nine

From "Me" to "Mom"— The Most Wonderful Time in Your Life Myth

The Most Wonderful Time in Your Life— Myth or Reality?

I am sure you have heard this one: "Now you have everything you have ever wanted. Isn't it wonderful?" The problem with this idea is that it is so inclusive. It leaves no room for the reality of the stresses of life with a new baby. Yes, there are many wonderful things about learning to care for and love your new baby. But at times it is difficult to balance the joy with the loss of self, freedom, time, spontaneity and sleep. One word to the wise new mom: nothing can be 100 percent wonderful. So enjoy the pleasant moments, and do not fret if they are not constant.

My name is Annette Brigham.
I am a hairstylist and the proud mother
of a beautiful little girl.

Baby's Name: _Janerica_

Date of Birth: _April 28, 1998_

Time of Birth: _4:05 P.M._

Weight: _5 pounds, 7 ounces_

Length: _17 ³/₄ inches_

My heart still beats fast every time I think about the day I left my newborn baby home alone. I adopted Janerica when she was two weeks old. We had been together about seven days when I made a terrible mistake. The tremendous guilt I felt then still pains me to this day. I must admit leaving my baby home alone is the one thing I've done that I am not proud of since becoming a new mother. But it is my story, one I've never shared with anyone before now. The reason I'm telling you what happened is because I don't want you or any other mother to experience the trauma I went through.

> *I couldn't believe I had given my baby a bath, put her clothes on—and then left the house without her! When I realized I had left her home alone I just panicked. I lost it.*
>
> —ANNETTE BRIGHAM

I was at home one morning when suddenly the telephone rang. My girlfriends were calling to invite me out for a day of shopping at a local mall. Of course, I said yes. I always welcomed an opportunity to hang out with my friends. We were very close—like sisters—and had been for years. All they had to do was say, "Let's," and I'd say, "Go," and we were gone. Excited, I jumped out of bed, took a shower and got dressed. I fed my daughter, Janerica, gave her a bath, dressed her in a cute frilly dress and laid her down in the middle of my bed.

Looking at my watch I realized I was going to be late

meeting my girlfriends if I didn't hurry. I rushed to the bathroom to comb my hair and put on some makeup. By the time
I was finished applying blush to my cheeks my pager beeped.
I checked the number and recognized the ten digits right
away. They belonged to one of my girlfriends. I didn't waste
time responding to her page because I knew she was only
wondering whether I was on my way. I grabbed my purse,
threw it over my shoulder and hurried out the door.

I got into my car, turned on the radio and drove down the
street heading to the mall. I had driven about a mile away
from my apartment when I looked in the rearview mirror and
saw an empty infant car seat. My heart sank immediately. I
couldn't believe I had given my baby a bath, put her clothes
on—and then left the house without her! When I realized I
had left her home alone I just panicked. I lost it. My chest was
hurting, and my heart was beating so fast I thought I was
going to have a heart attack. All I could think about was getting back home to my baby.

My eyes glistened with moisture, but the tears wouldn't
fall. I wanted to cry, but I couldn't. I guess I was too scared. I
started driving very fast like a crazy woman. I was afraid the
police were going to stop me, and if they did, and I told them
why I was speeding, they would arrest me, charge me with
child abandonment or child cruelty, and take my baby away
from me. I had never been so scared before in my life. As I
was driving, all sorts of thoughts about my baby ran through
my mind. I kept thinking Janerica had rolled over and fallen
out of the bed. I could see her lying on the floor, hurt and

crying, with no one to hear her. I can't tell you how frightened I was. I started praying, asking the Lord to protect my baby.

When I finally got home, my heart was racing and my hands were sweating and trembling so badly I couldn't open the door. I dropped the keys on the ground once or twice before I finally stuck the right one into the lock, turned it and opened the door. I bolted through it like lightning, ran straight to my bedroom and found Janerica lying in the middle of the bed where I had left her. She was sound asleep. I took a deep breath and collapsed on the floor right then and there. I fell on my knees and thanked the Lord for watching over my baby.

As reality began to sink in, I still couldn't believe I had left Janerica home alone. When I thought about how much I loved her and how long I had waited to get her I felt so much pain and guilt. I beat myself up for not being a good mother. All I could do was hold my face in my hands and ask for her forgiveness. When I finally calmed down and regained composure, I kissed my baby on her cheek, rubbed her back and apologized for leaving her alone. I also promised her I would never make that mistake again. And I haven't.

Moments later, I sat on the floor beside the bed and had a long talk with myself. "I have to start thinking like a mother," I murmured under my breath. I had to accept the fact that my life wasn't just about me and only me anymore. That was hard for me to accept initially. Because I had been single and living alone for so long, I had never had to think about anyone except me. I was in my own self-centered world—definitely in a "me" frame of mind. It was painfully clear that I needed to reprogram myself and make a transition to a "mother" frame of mind. But because I had never been a mother before, I wasn't quite sure how to do that.

After thinking long and hard, I realized that in addition to my many roles I had to add "mother" to the list that describes who I am. I had to lavish my baby with love, protect her and be a mother to her. I have been blessed with a beautiful baby girl who I love with all my heart. I know I have to take care of her and be responsible for her in every way—especially making sure she is safe and never leaving her home alone. I learned that lesson the hard way, but it was a lesson well learned. In fact, to make sure I never leave my baby home alone again, I leave her diapers and diaper bag at the front door so that I will see them when I prepare to leave. That works like a charm!

Annette's Savvy Strategies

- When you make a mistake, ask for forgiveness—and forgive yourself. You are only human!
- Repacking the diaper bag each time you come in means you can be much more spontaneous about flying out the door on the next trip.

Analysis about Annette's story follows stories of Michelle and Tracy. All three stories take a closer look at women making the transition to thinking about themselves as mothers.

My name is Michelle Goldsmith.
I am a teacher and the proud mother
of a beautiful little girl.

Baby's Name: *Paige Alexa*

Date of Birth: *April 28, 1999*

Time of Birth: *5:00 P.M.*

Weight: *7 pounds, 15 ounces*

Length: *20 inches*

I was very lonely when I first brought my baby home from the hospital. It was a strange feeling, completely foreign to me. I felt like my soul was empty, and I didn't know how to fill the void. The fact that I was terribly lonesome, even though I had my beautiful baby girl with me, was awfully perplexing. It left me feeling sad, guilty and confused.

Just after Paige was born, I was euphoric and couldn't wait to strengthen our bond—something I had envisioned during my pregnancy. When my husband and I brought

Paige would sleep for at least three hours at a time. That's when I really felt the sting of loneliness—nothing to do, no one to talk with.

—MICHELLE GOLDSMITH

her home from the hospital I did not want anyone else around. I wanted us to have a wonderful time bonding as a family— just the three of us. I was adamant about that because it was what I had imagined for months. It was such an intensely personal time, and I felt like that was family time, our time.

Things were going as well as could be expected until my husband returned to work and left Paige and me home alone. All of a sudden I felt lonely—not something I had imagined, and not something I understood. Paige was such a good baby. All she did was sleep, eat and poop. I nursed her every three to four hours, changed her diapers and put her down to nap. I loved performing these mothering tasks and enjoyed them immensely. Paige would sleep for at least three hours at a time. That's when I really felt the sting of loneliness— nothing to do, no one to talk with. And our house was quiet— very quiet. I hadn't noticed the silence before because I was always on the go.

Being a third-grade teacher I had always had plenty to keep me busy. My day usually started around 5:30 A.M. After a shower and breakfast, I grabbed my keys, hit the road and arrived at school at about 7:00 A.M., ready to teach the three Rs all day. Between classes, I planned assignments, graded papers and visited colleagues. After school, I attended staff meetings, went to aerobics, prepared dinner and dined with my husband. Sometimes we went out for a bite or to a movie or both. Later I would relax: curl up with my favorite book or magazine, then shower and called it a night at about 10:30 P.M. I repeated the same routine day after day with only slight variations.

When Paige arrived, however, that all changed. Oh sure, I was busy performing mothering tasks that I welcomed, and I had to deal with bouts of exhaustion, but I wasn't nearly as busy as I was before. Being home with Paige all day made me feel as though I was not accomplishing as much as I used to. I felt guilty and very confused by my reaction to mothering: I absolutely love my baby, and I have a burning passion for children. I have been around kids all of my life, and I love nurturing and educating them.

I grasped at everything I could think of to end the lone-liness. I sent e-mails, read baby books and magazines, and watched soap operas on television. I also took naps—occasionally. I felt vulnerable and yearned to talk with my friends about the number-one movie at the box office, the big class project or how my students were excelling, but all my friends were working. Needless to say, I missed socializing with them tremendously. None of my girlfriends had babies, and they were always on the move. I felt like I was missing out, like I was the only one in my situation—sitting home embraced by loneliness. That was hard for me to deal with emotionally, harder than I expected, really.

I figured it was hard for me to be home with Paige because she didn't talk, she didn't have much of a personality and she didn't smile. And, she couldn't go out in public for six weeks—as doctors tell all moms—to prevent her from catching germs. So we stayed inside. Occasionally I found myself wondering how other mothers were coping. How were they handling cabin fever? Sometimes I dreamed about sharing adventures with Paige—going to the park or to the zoo and having the kind of fun outings moms look forward to doing with their babies.

After six weeks of my feeling lonely, Paige was old enough to venture out and leave the comforts of home. I wondered what we would do first—go to the park, go shopping, or visit friends and family. As luck would have it, a colleague from school called to invite me to the annual teachers' overnight retreat. I couldn't stand the thought of not going. The retreats were so much fun. They were held on a huge ranch. All of my friends would be there, including one of my best friends with whom I had roomed for five years. I was still on maternity leave and school officials didn't expect me to attend the event, but I had to: I needed to go.

I discussed the retreat with my husband who was very supportive and understanding of my feelings. We decided I should go and take Paige with me. I was still nursing her at the time and couldn't stand the idea of being away from her. The trip turned out to be a lifesaver for me. I had a great time. I was surrounded by all of my friends, having adult conversations, doing fun things—and everyone wanted to hold Paige and shower her with love and affection.

The retreat exceeded my expectations. One night I was in my room getting Paige ready for bed, and I realized I didn't feel lonely anymore. Loneliness had left me. Poof—like magic, it was gone. I was so happy. I was exhilarated for the duration of the trip. When Paige and I returned home I was still blissfully happy, and I didn't feel lonely anymore when we were alone. Of course, it didn't take much for me to realize that during those times when I felt like I wasn't accomplishing much I had been doing quite a lot. I was so fortunate to be home with my baby: loving her, caring for her and bonding with her. I'm incredibly grateful for that.

A year after the retreat, I made a painful decision. I decided to give up my flourishing teaching career to stay home with Paige full time. It was a very tough decision to make because I love education, and I felt an obligation to my students. But I wanted to spend more time with my baby to nurture her and watch her grow. I didn't want to miss out on the little things: when she said her first word, or when she took her first step. Since Paige was starting to talk, to develop her own personality and to get into everything, I found it a lot easier to be alone with her. Plus, I made friends with other new moms and participated in various activities for mothers and babies. Suffice it to say, I was so busy I didn't have time to be lonely.

Michelle's Savvy Strategies

- Connect with the "pre-baby" parts of yourself as soon as you can. Resume some fun activity or social activity that does not require you to be a mom.
- Connect with other moms—a great source of validation and enrichment for your life.

Analysis of Michelle's story will follow Tracy's story about her transition to "feeling like a mom."

My name is Tracy Bice.
I am a stay-at-home mom and the
proud mother of beautiful
identical twin boys.

Baby's Name: *William Robert*

Date of Birth: *Dec. 9, 2000*

Time of Birth: *11:00 A.M.*

Weight: *3 pounds, 11 ounces*

Length: *16 inches*

Baby's Name: *Ryan Neal*

Date of Birth: *Dec. 9, 2000*

Time of Birth: *11:01 A.M.*

Weight: *4 pounds, 2 ounces*

Length: *15 inches*

I always rely on my faith in God to get me through the day. It doesn't matter whether I encounter bleak or beautiful circumstances. No matter what I'm going through I pray about it and put my trust in the Lord. That was how I was raised. I was born into a religious family. My parents are devout Roman Catholics. When I was a young girl I adopted their beliefs wholeheartedly. I went to Mass regularly and practiced every ritual of my religion. I still do.

When I was growing up, my parents told me if I ever needed anything, to go to God in prayer because he is always

> *Having to depend on someone else was hard for me to accept initially because I was a very stubborn, independent woman.*
>
> —TRACY BICE

there. I grew in his spirit quickly and didn't hesitate to call on him. When I took exams in school, I prayed. When I graduated from high school and wondered what to do with my life, I prayed. When I finished college and started teaching junior high students, I prayed. And when I found the love of my life and we decided to marry, I prayed.

So it was only natural that I prayed when I discovered I was pregnant—with twins. I was twelve weeks into my pregnancy when a sonogram revealed the wonderful yet stunning news. My husband and I couldn't believe it. No one in our family had twins. We had not done anything medically to enhance our chances of having twins. We were not prepared for twins. It's no wonder, when the doctor told us I was carrying two babies, that we were shocked into shouting "Oh my gosh!" repeatedly as if we had won a multi million-dollar lottery.

My pregnancy was going extremely well until I reached the third trimester. That's when things started going downhill. By that time I had gained sixty pounds. I also had difficulty breathing, and I had a rare pregnancy rash called Pupps. Talk about discomfort! It was the most horrible thing I ever had to deal with. The rash covered my entire body. It was red, scaly, and itchy, and it forced me out of bed in the middle of the night more times than I care to remember. I took cold oatmeal baths, hoping they would soothe my skin. They didn't. Unrelenting discomfort forced me to visit a dermatologist who gave me steroid shots every three weeks. They provided much needed relief from the itching, but the rash didn't go away until I delivered my babies—two and a half months early. The real comfort was not experiencing any side effects. Protecting my unborn twins from harm was of the utmost importance to me.

In hindsight, my babies probably came early because I was under a lot of stress at the time. My dad had been diagnosed with colon cancer. He had surgery on a Monday, and contractions forced me to the hospital the following Thursday. My doctor tried to stop the labor by giving me magnesium sulfate. That worked for a day, but by Friday night I started having contractions again. When Saturday rolled around my doctor examined me again and then blurted, "Let's go have these guys." When he said that I had an immediate emotional rush that brought tears to my eyes. I kept thinking, *They're not ready yet.* My mind was consumed with thoughts of what could go wrong because my babies were going to be born early—too early. Needless to say, I was very concerned about their health, especially their lungs. Of course, I was hopeful and prayerful.

When William's high-pitched voice overpowered the delivery room I felt a great sense of relief—it was an indication that his lungs were nice and strong. The sheer volume of his voice pushed my worries aside. A nurse brought my precious baby to me. Melting, I kissed his beautiful face and marveled at him for only a few seconds before she whisked him away to the neonatal intensive care unit (NICU). A minute later, Ryan made a quiet entrance into the world. Fear gripped me quickly. The worry that had vanished after William was born reappeared more intensely. I feared something was urgently wrong with my baby. His lungs—were they strong enough? It bothered me that Ryan didn't make a loud rousing announcement the way his brother had done only a moment before. His silence captured my attention and forced my heart to pound rapidly. A group of doctors and nurses worked feverishly with Ryan to get him breathing. Within seconds, they accomplished their mission. Ryan was placed in an incubator and rushed to the NICU just as his brother had been a short time before. The scenario was oddly different. Even worse, I didn't get to meet my precious baby.

While I didn't get to greet Ryan, to touch him or kiss him, I understood that his needs were urgent and took precedence over my yearning to hold him. A short time later, however, I received great news: I could visit my babies. While I was lying comfortably in bed, a nurse wheeled me slowly to the NICU. My eyes searched the room quickly until they found Ryan. He was lying in an incubator sleeping under small heat lamps. I still wasn't allowed to hold him, but I could touch him. I slid my index finger inside Ryan's tiny hand, and he squeezed it gently. It was a tender moment, and I cherished it immensely.

On an emotional high, I rejoiced as the nurse pushed my bed down a short hall so that I could visit William. Different medical needs forced the separation of my boys. William was underweight and jaundiced; Ryan was jaundiced, underweight and had trouble breathing. Like his brother, William was sound asleep, resting comfortably under soft heat lamps in his incubator. I extended my hand and stroked his arm gently, being careful not to overstimulate him. His skin was amazingly soft—like cotton.

Two weeks later, my babies were moved into the same room in the NICU and placed in the same bed. It was incredibly moving to see them snuggled up next to each other. I took comfort knowing William and Ryan were together again, much like they had been when I carried them. Even though they were attached to intravenous (IV) tubes, and to machines that monitored their heart rate and breathing, it didn't take away from the joy I felt. I fell in love with them instantly, and prayed they would be healthy enough to leave the NICU as soon as possible.

I was released from the hospital long before William and Ryan were—three days after I delivered them, in fact. I wasn't surprised. I knew the time would come when I would be released, and they would have to stay. At my discharge, however, I had a hard time leaving my babies. I wanted to be with them all the time—to hold them, feed them and love them. Instead of fulfilling my storybook dream of going home with my babies, I went home empty-handed. That was one of the hardest things I ever had to do.

Regular trips to the hospital helped ease my pain. My husband and I visited William and Ryan every day, three or four times a day. I pumped milk and took it along during our visits to feed our babies. I was proud of the fact that I was fulfilling such a vital motherly role—providing their nourishment. That also helped lift my spirits.

The staff of nurses in the NICU went to great lengths to make sure my husband and I did as much as we could for our babies on our own. But they were always in close proximity just in case we needed them—we needed them a lot. I was nervous initially about changing William and Ryan. I was scared to touch them because they were so tender and tiny and attached to so many tubes. The nurses were extremely helpful and made caring for our twins less stressful. They taught us how to take their temperature, feed them and change their diapers. And they encouraged us. "You can do it," they would say.

I remember carefully sliding my hands into a set of plastic gloves attached to two small holes in the side of the boys' incubator. Then I worked around the lifelines that were attached to my babies at one end and to monitors that tracked their heart rate and breathing at the other. I was careful not to shake William and Ryan too much or detach the monitors' electrodes that were glued to their chests. After a slight struggle, I managed with trembling hands to change their diapers. Sound the trumpet: That was a triumphant moment!

The nurses also taught me little things that made a big difference, like how to gently stroke the boys' heads to make them burp. I know that sounds strange, but it works. They also taught me how to give my babies sponge baths separately—it was safer—and how to stack them one on top of the other, cradle them in my arm like footballs and rock them. Holding William and Ryan together like that and feeling their little bodies next to mine made mothering very real to me.

Sometimes, after visiting my babies, I would go home and think about caring for them and warm tears would flow from my eyes. I would get so emotional that if my husband looked at me a certain way I would lose it. I think being so emotional was caused in part by my serious doubts about my mothering skills. Even though I received a lot of help from the nurses, I felt like I couldn't handle motherhood.

After gaining about two pounds each, William and Ryan were finally released from the hospital—seven weeks after they were born. I didn't know how to respond. I was glad to finally take my babies home, but I was also sad to leave the hospital. The nurses who had provided so much encouragement and who had taught me so much about caring for my babies were not coming home with us. No longer would I be under their watchful eyes.

William and Ryan were still attached to monitors when I brought them home. I was excited, nervous and fearful at the same time. I was terribly afraid to be left alone with my babies because I didn't think I could care for them properly. I watched them very closely every second. And their monitors—a habit I had developed while they were in the NICU. Every now and again the alarms would sound indicating that their heart rates had dropped or they had stopped breathing. That usually happened during feedings when they got very relaxed. The alarms struck fear in my heart, but there was little time for fear or panic in those situations—only quick reaction. A gentle rub on my babies' legs or arms usually triggered a positive response and got them back to normal.

Bathing the boys was another challenge. My husband and I devised a system that worked well for us. We undressed, bathed and redressed one baby. Then we grabbed the other one and repeated the process. Everything was definitely a team effort, even feedings. I started out breastfeeding William and Ryan at the same time—once every three hours. I quickly discovered, however, that I didn't have enough hands to do the job properly. My babies wouldn't latch on at the same time: one would fall off while the other was nursing without incident. Then my husband would try to hold the baby who was successfully nursing in place while I struggled to get the other one latched on again. It was exhausting, uncomfortable and frustrating.

I kept telling my husband, "This is not the way it's supposed to be." Yet the same scenario played out for about seven weeks. I finally surrendered to frustration and stopped breastfeeding

William and Ryan. I felt guilty, like I had bonded with my breast pump instead of with my twins. Not breastfeeding them while they were in the hospital may also have forced those emotions to surface. I reverted back to the ritual I had started when my babies were in the NICU. I pumped milk, put it in bottles and then fed my boys. That worked out better for all of us.

Diapering my boys wasn't nearly as bad as feeding them. In fact, it was easy by comparison. But my babies went through a lot of diapers—at least fifteen to seventeen a day. There were times I fell victim to exhaustion, but I tapped into my reserve energy and kept plugging along. Caring for twins didn't give me any time for dwelling on sleep or a lack of it. I had really lost a lot of sleep by the time my husband was ready to return to work. He had taken time off from his construction job when our babies were born, but when it was time for him to return, I wanted him to quit and stay home with me instead. Yes, I knew my husband needed to work to support us. At the time, however, his earning a living was not a priority to me. I was too wrapped up in my own fears to think rationally.

It pained me to ask my husband to stay home and help me look after our twins. I thought I would be able to handle the load alone, but caring for my boys by myself proved to be too much. Having to depend on someone else to help me care for William and Ryan was hard for me to accept initially because I had always been a very stubborn, independent woman. I had bought my own car and my own house, and I had a thriving career long before I walked down the aisle and said, "I do."

Parenting in that era was much more of a community endeavor, with women helping each other out. This provided in a very practical way the proverbial "village" that it takes to raise a child. Tracy might not have felt like she had to handle her babies all on her own. Michelle certainly would have felt much less lonely in such a setting. And Annette might have had Grandma living in the upstairs bedroom, so when she dashed out the door, Janerica would not have been alone.

In today's world, however, neighborhoods more often than not have a very isolated atmosphere. Women are expected to "do it all" on their own. When I had my first baby no one else on my street had children. I knew no one who stayed home all day. Michelle's social isolation and loneliness, Annette's crisis and Tracy's independent streak are all a product of our increasingly mobile society. If you are dealing with the isolation that caring for an infant brings, know that new mothers are still out there. You may just need to look a lot harder to find them, using new skills and technologies. Check out these options:

- The Internet: Chat rooms for parents are extremely popular; they meet the need that all new parents have for social support.
- New mom and baby exercise groups—found at hospitals, health clubs, municipal recreation centers.
- Support groups provided by hospitals, mental health associations, the La Leche League and religious institutions.
- Baby gym or music classes offered by Little Gym, Kindermusik, Gymboree and others.

- Babysitting cooperatives—often found within home-
owners' or tenants' associations.
- Organize your own group. Post notices at the pediatrician's office, the local health clinic, the local baby super-
store. Meet at a park or other neutral setting.

All of these types of groups have evolved to meet this need for social support. New mothers are less likely to experience postpartum depression if they have friends who also have small children or infants. Michelle felt a lot better about her new role when she began to connect with other new moms, thus resuming her old "social" self.

The Wonderful Time Myth

A huge cultural myth about becoming a mother is illus-
trated in both Michelle's and Tracy's stories. As a culture, we inundate new mothers with the idea that "this is the most won-
derful time of your life." We see print advertisements, TV commercials and programs that show smiling parents and babies playing. It all looks like such fun! How could a new mom ever get lonely with this nonstop interaction with a glowing baby? Why would she want to have an afternoon off, or time to herself, if this is so wonderful?

Go beyond the myth to the reality with a newborn and the explanation is clear. Babies sleep a great deal; they cry a great deal. Their responses are pretty basic in this way. Newborns are not very good at feedback other than crying. They cannot carry on a conversation or laugh at your jokes. Babies simply are not very social for the first three months of life. It is hard to just strap them in the car and head off on an adventure, even if the adventure is only to the grocery store. Everything about them seems to take lots of time. And if you have never had a baby before, this reality is in high contrast to what our cultural myths may have led you to believe.

The Totality Myth

Similarly, do not be deceived by the totality myth. The totality myth leads women to believe that loving the baby and loving the job go hand in hand. Michelle loved Paige. The job was just not what she imagined. New mothers can feel both these ways at once. They can love their babies and be glad they have them. And they can also hate the day-to-day drudgery and isolation. Drop the idea that because you wanted this baby badly you must also adore every single aspect of your new life with the baby. You can love the baby and still hate the job.

Reassurance in the Ever-Changing Nature of the Job

Michelle simply was falling prey to these unrealistic expectations about what kind of company a newborn baby really is. With time, she discovered that Paige did indeed grow into a much more social creature—pleased to laugh at and coo with her mom. Then the fun really began. Keep in mind that many women have distinct preferences for certain stages in a child's life. Some really love the newborn stage, with a baby snuggled into their shoulder sleepily. Others find it much more fun to have an older baby who can laugh and coo.

Still some mothers much prefer a three-year-old who can relate his day at preschool. There is nothing wrong with you if you find babyhood trying, or would trade your newborn for a six-year-old any day. If your child is at a stage you abhor, take heart. Not only will your child enter another stage soon—you need only wait a brief while—but you can still be a good enough parent even when you are not thrilled with this current stage of development.

For Tracy, adapting to the demands of two babies, and the fact that she really needed help, eventually allowed her to relinquish her unrealistic expectation that she was the "only one who can care for my babies." She may have had a slow start coming to terms with this because her babies were in the NICU first, and so she had breaks and help built into her routine. She knew she needed that then, because her babies required specialized medical care.

Once the babies came home, she overlooked a basic truth: that taking care of one newborn is a full-time job, so taking care of twins alone is like juggling double overtime. Much like Donna, she was used to being independent and "doing it all," so this was new territory. Eventually, her own needs won out. The simple things like a shower or a shopping trip along with valid anxiety about her babies' medical demands finally triumphed.

New mothers need mothering themselves. If you are continually giving to others, you are emptying out your emotional bank account. If you do nothing to fill it up again, pretty soon you are overdrawn. Then you have nothing left to give. All new mothers need to refill their accounts. Make Shirley's "mommy moments" for yourself. Accept assistance from any willing, trustworthy hands. Then you will continue to have resources to give to your children.

Annette's story illustrates another common theme found in Cheryl Beck's research on new mothers. This is an inability to concentrate, dubbed "the fog." The combination of fluctuating hormones, sleep deprivation and the sheer load of caring for a newborn twenty-four hours a day, seven days a week, makes the new mother feel fuzzy and confused at times. Faced with

"Mommy Moments" and "The Fog"

The fog many new mothers feel is primarily related to sleep deprivation. When you begin to get more sleep, the fog may lessen. Many new mothers find that the fog continues as long as they have small children. Multiple schedules and demands, and zillions of things to remember, all contribute to the fact that you simply cannot think as clearly as you did before you had children. Some "experts" suggest that this is because of the theory of the "conservation of intelligence." Tongue in cheek, this theory proposes that each family is allotted only so many IQ points. As children get smarter, parents get dumber! What can actually help with this feeling of fogginess is taking some time for yourself, each day and certainly each week. "Mommy moments," in which you do what you want, can be as simple as spending five minutes . . .

- Listening to one song on a favorite CD
- Talking to a friend on the phone
- Deep breathing
- Enjoying a cup of tea
- Reading one magazine article

Make yourself a list of your "Five-Minute Favorites," and post it on the fridge as a reminder to take a moment for you.

distraction, as Annette was when her pager went off, new mothers frequently forgot what track they were on. They may forget to put the laundry in the dryer, finding it a day later all crumpled, beginning to mildew. They may lose the car keys or burn the rice. In this case, Annette dashed out the door without her daughter. The fog is normal, and it does disappear when the new mother begins to get more sleep.

Other strategies can prevent possible tragedies, such as those Annette imagined as she rushed home to her infant. Self-talk is one, and it can take many forms: "Think like a mom, think like a mom," or "I walked back here to get a diaper." Just repeat to yourself whatever you wish to remember. Reminder lists and notes are also helpful, as was Annette's strategy of leaving the diaper bag by the front door. With time and this kind of self-talk, you, too, can "think like a mom."

Ten

Letting Go—
The Mother Always
Makes It Better
Myth

Mother Always Makes It Better— Myth or Reality?

When we were children, who always made it better? Mom, of course. From skinned knees to being dumped by our first love, Mom always seemed to know just what to do to soothe us. Now that we are mothers, we expect to have the same kind of powers. We think we can control everything, make it all "okay" for our children. Soon, however, the reality about our lack of control sets in.

My name is Lori Morris.
I am a certified recreational therapist
and the proud mother of a beautiful little girl.

Baby's Name: *Sarah Ann*

Date of Birth: *July 7, 2000*

Time of Birth: *3:09 A.M.*

Weight: *8 pounds, 13 ounces*

Length: *21 inches*

I had an insatiable appetite for carrots when I was pregnant. I craved those sweet, orange, crunchy vegetables every day throughout my pregnancy, and I ate them at the same time every morning during staff meetings. It was the weirdest thing. When the clock struck eleven, I instinctively whipped out a bag of carrots. My colleagues got a kick out of my routine and teased me about my eating habits. I didn't mind their lighthearted ribbing because I was proud of myself for eating healthy food for me and for my baby.

> *The first night we were home, Sarah screamed her head off. She was totally miserable. The broccoli I had eaten affected her terribly.*
>
> —LORI MORRIS

I was a good eater before I became pregnant. After I learned I was pregnant, however, I became an even better eater. I was very conscientious about the food I ate and made sure I had good, nutritious meals. I also exercised throughout my pregnancy: I walked almost every day and swam three times a week. The combination of eating healthy foods and exercising helped keep my weight down, too. I only gained twenty-six pounds when I was pregnant.

During my third trimester I felt a little pelvic pressure from my baby's weight, and I bought a girdle-support belt, which helped alleviate some of the discomfort. Other than that, I did not experience a lot of pressure, pain or swelling. Toward the very end of my pregnancy, however, my baby was sitting on a nerve in my left leg, and that caused the leg to do some strange things. Sometimes when I walked my foot would flop around like a fish out of water. During the last week of my pregnancy, the leg would be numb by the end of my workday. It wasn't painful, just irritating. All things considered, these were minor inconveniences, and I didn't let them bother me because my pregnancy was going very well.

My situation changed dramatically when I went into labor. About three hours after my first contraction, I got an epidural. A nurse broke my water, and my baby began moving very rapidly down the birth canal. At the same time, the members of the medical team started losing her heartbeat. When that happened, my husband was told to leave the delivery room and slip into a pair of scrubs immediately. Someone put an oxygen mask on my face, and another member of the team began shaking my belly, tapping on it and moving it from side to side, trying to stir my baby.

I heard someone yell for a room to do an emergency C-section. I was very worried—especially because no one had been able to locate my doctor. Suddenly, he appeared out of nowhere. The minute he walked into the delivery room my baby's heartbeat bounced back up to a normal rhythm. After pushing for about an hour, my beautiful baby girl was born.

I didn't get to hold Sarah for about forty-five minutes because of the heartbeat scare. That was disappointing because I thought I would meet her right away. A delivery nurse took Sarah to a warming table to examine her and record her Apgar scores. Lying on the delivery table, I took comfort watching my husband interact with Sarah. He had held only one or two babies in his life up until our daughter was born. I was so proud of him and felt warm all over when he put Sarah's first diaper on, and he calmed her down with his soothing voice.

When the nurse asked my husband if he wanted to carry our baby over to me, however, I said, "Oh, no. Don't let him carry her! Not across the room! He doesn't have any experience carrying babies!" I panicked because I thought my husband was going to drop Sarah. Thank goodness he managed to carry her across the delivery room and hand her to me without incident. That was really special.

When I looked at my beautiful little girl's sweet face it was an extraordinary feeling. It seemed so surreal: I had carried her and taken care of her for nine months, talking to her and reassuring her; she had kicked and poked me, letting me know she was going to make her debut soon; I had been very aware of her existence. Now she was "here," and when I held her for the first time, all I could do was stare at her.

Amid the joy there was one slight irritation. Believe it or not, I was upset about the food I was served in the hospital after Sarah was born. I was given spicy beef one night and spicy barbecue the next. For breakfast I was given fried eggs with greasy, spicy sausage. I couldn't believe it. Needless to say, I didn't eat any of the food because I was nursing. I didn't want to pass along anything to Sarah that would upset her stomach. I remember thinking, *I'm in a maternity ward. This food is absolutely inappropriate. I need bland food.*

The night before I took Sarah home, I must have taken leave of my senses because I ate a helping of broccoli I was served for dinner. That was totally dumb on my part. I knew better than to eat broccoli, of all things, when I was nursing. It didn't take long for problems to start. The first night we were home, Sarah screamed her head off. She was totally miserable. The broccoli I had eaten affected her terribly.

In a flash, my mind raced back to how carefully I had eaten during my pregnancy, and now I had made this terrible mistake. Listening to my baby scream was unbearable. I could tell she was very uncomfortable, and I didn't know what to do to make her feel better. I just held her. I didn't cry, but I sure felt like crying. I kept beating myself up and mumbling under my breath, "I could have prevented this." Even though I knew I didn't cause Sarah's pain intentionally, I felt horrible.

I kept asking myself, *How could you do this to Sarah?* She was such a good baby. Sarah nursed right from the beginning without any problems. I was so proud of her because I had been afraid that she wouldn't latch on. I had heard so many horror stories about how difficult nursing can be, how some babies never latch on. But she didn't have that problem. I had a hard time forgiving myself for what I had done to Sarah. I kept telling her over and over how sorry I was.

Determined to ease Sarah's pain, I quickly scanned a brochure about caring for babies that the hospital had given me. According to the brochure, if an infant's bowel movement has a bad odor, there could be a problem. Sarah's was very, very stinky. I called the hospital and a nurse suggested I call the doctor if her movements continued to have an odor. Fortunately, it did not take long for the broccoli to pass through Sarah's system. By noon the following day she was fine.

Sarah had a few more colicky episodes. Even though I watched what I ate closely, she still got an upset stomach every now and again. When Sarah cried, her screams went through me. At that point, my husband believed in letting her cry it out. He persuaded me to leave Sarah in her nursery to cry. After about five minutes I couldn't take it anymore. "I don't care what you say," I told my husband. "Enough is enough. I'm getting my baby."

I didn't think I would have a problem letting Sarah cry because I had to do that with babies when I babysat. But when it was my own child it really bothered me. I couldn't do it. Like all couples, my husband and I have our disagreements about what's best for our baby. We try to discuss each situation and make the best decisions possible. Sometimes when Sarah is crying, I have to go to her no matter what.

Right before I went back to work, Sarah had another crying spell. She wouldn't stop screaming. I held her and rocked her, but I was so emotional I had to put her down and go outside. I stood on my front porch and cried like a baby. I was outside crying, and Sarah was inside crying. We were quite a pair. My misery was compounded by the fact that I had to return to work the following day, and I didn't want to leave Sarah. I kept thinking, *I've been home with her for three months. I've spent every single moment with her. And now I've got to leave her.* I was not comfortable with that at all.

I knew Sarah was going to get excellent care at the day care center I had selected. But the thought of leaving her with someone else was very difficult for me to handle. In fact, the first day I took Sarah to day care was horrible. She did very well. I was a basket case. I had gotten halfway to the facility when I thought, *I'm doing well. Better than I thought.* At that very moment, I started bawling. I walked into the day care center crying my eyes out. I startled Sarah's child care provider who was very concerned. Through uncontrollable sobs, I tried to explain to her that I was having a hard time letting go, and then I tried explain what was in Sarah's diaper bag. After I left, I cried for about an hour.

In the midst of my gloom, I decided to work half days for the first week. It was important for me to gradually move back into my routine. Taking things slowly helped me get used to being separated from Sarah. While I still miss my baby something awful when I'm not with her, I can better deal with the separation. And knowing I'll see Sarah after work gives me something special to look forward to at the end of my business day.

> ## Lori's Savvy Strategies
>
> • Take things slowly and allow time for adjustment.
> • Be vigilant about those parts of your life you can control.

Lori's story is a good example of letting go. An analysis of her experience follows Terri's and Leisa's stories about giving up the illusion of control in your baby's life.

My name is Terri Brown.
I am a teacher, writer and the proud mother
of a beautiful little girl.

Baby's Name: _Isabel Adele_

Date of Birth: _October 15, 1997_

Time of Birth: _5:50 P.M._

Weight: _2 pounds, 9 ounces_

Length: _11 3/4 inches_

I felt hollow when I came home from the hospital without my baby. After all the imagined scenes of coming home together, I never expected to feel such emptiness. I was devastated. My daughter Isabel was born prematurely and had medical problems—it would be weeks before I could bring her home. That a flock of substitute mothers and fathers would be holding her instead of my husband and me weighed heavily on my mind.

In hindsight, I was in no condition to care for my baby because I was recovering from a serious bout of preeclampsia (pregnancy-related high blood pressure and swelling). I was twenty-eight weeks into my pregnancy when I was diagnosed with the condition. I went to see my obstetrician for my regularly scheduled appointment. During my examination he tapped my knee with his medical hammer, and I gave him a swift kick in the head. Hyper-reflexes are common for preeclamptic mothers. My reflexes were very strong, and my blood pressure was sky high. My doctor sent me home on bed rest to await the results of an ultrasound—my second during the pregnancy. Elevated blood pressure coupled with little amniotic fluid and my baby's slowed growth sent me to the hospital the next day. I was told I would be there until my baby was born. So much for an easy pregnancy.

The radiologist told me my baby had to be born that day. After weeks of relative calm, I cried quite a bit that morning.

—Terri Brown

After three weeks of lying on my right side and receiving steroid injections, the routine fetal monitoring showed my baby's heart rate was dropping. A sonogram revealed the amniotic fluid had disappeared altogether. My radiologist told me my baby had to be born that day. After weeks of relative calm, I cried quite a bit that morning. I knew my child's prospects of survival were quite good, but beyond that I also knew potential problems were numerous.

Before I was prepped for the C-section, I asked to meet with one of the staff neonatologists. Strapped to an oxygen mask, I could barely hear him as he read through a list of maladies that could possibly afflict our soon-to-be-born child. My physician-husband and I were already familiar with the numbing list. Lung development was, of course, our primary concern, and cerebral palsy was a real possibility.

The neonatologist's final comment was stinging and made us feel even more helpless. His voice swelled with hope when he asked, "Do you know the sex of the baby?" Unfortunately we did not. My husband and I wanted to be surprised by the birth of our first child. "Let's hope it's a girl," the neonatologist continued.

"Well, there's not much we can do about that one now, can we," I replied. We knew in this situation that the baby's sex was important: Girls had a small edge over boys because their organs developed earlier prenatally.

As I headed into surgery I tried to be optimistic, but I was scared. The nurses attempted to reassure me. They kept saying, "Your baby is thirty-one weeks. She's going to be fine." I was touched by their compassion and took comfort knowing they had met a lot of mothers of preemies. Still, it was hard to dismiss the possible outcomes for my infant.

There was quite a team in the operating room, including two obstetricians and a neonatologist. Heavily medicated, I barely remember the delivery, but the birth was speedy. My husband and I were a bit relieved at the first announcement: "You've got a baby girl." But the real wave of relief came with her bellowing. It was clear she had a good set of lungs. The neonatologist held our baby up for us to see—all mouth already—then dashed down the hall. All the news thus far was as good as we could expect. My nurse in the postoperating room was someone I knew well. She brought in a Polaroid and took a picture of our baby: She was all red and bony, but she was ours.

> ## HELLP Syndrome
>
> HELLP Syndrome is a rare but very serious complication of preeclampsia. It is a group of potentially life-threatening symptoms that include hemolytic anemia (H), elevated liver enzymes (EL) and a low platelet count (LP).

Before I was taken up to my room the next morning, I was wheeled to the Neonatal Intensive Care Unit (NICU). My daughter was lying in a small incubator being warmed by its soft beaming lights. I touched her hand gently. Our meeting wasn't quite like one of the tales of mother-baby bonding that you read about in baby care books, but I was grateful nonetheless. Little did I know that this would be the only visit I would have with her all week.

Preeclampsia usually goes away with birth, but mine worsened within twenty-four hours, developing into what is called

HELLP Syndrome. My platelet count was dropping, my blood pressure was still high, and I was developing some signs of kidney and liver malfunction. There would be no walking the halls for me. I didn't even have my epidural line pulled for a few days. Most important, I couldn't visit my daughter. I was crushed. The obstetricians were sympathetic but firm. I couldn't get out of bed. I was also told I couldn't begin to pump breast milk.

Needless to say, the "distance" between my newborn and me made motherhood seem all the more intangible. My sister and brother had seen my daughter more than I had, and so had my husband. He was terrific throughout the ordeal. He went to see Isabel in the nursery every day and held her in his arms for hours. He also gave me daily reports about her condition. I was comforted knowing Isabel was able to feel her father's warm touch.

After five days, I was given the okay to be wheeled to the NICU to get my chance to hold my baby. I scanned the rows of tiny newborns until my eyes landed on my beautiful daughter. Isabel was hooked up to a heart and apnea monitor, an intravenous line and a feeding tube. And, typical of most babies, she had lost weight. Since Isabel had weighed in at two pounds, nine ounces, there wasn't much to lose. She was still very red and her veins were just beneath the surface of her very thin skin. But I got to hold her, and I was told that I could change her diaper the next day. I was terrified, but the nurses in the unit were wonderfully reassuring.

However, adding to my hand wringing were Isabel's bouts

of bradycardia and apnea. She had been diagnosed with the conditions about 48 hours after she was born. Bradycardia is a drop in heart rate. With preemies it is usually caused by their underdevelopment. Isabel's heart rate dropped when she was overstimulated—or when she fell into a deep sleep. The apnea, the moments when she would stop breathing, was a bit more common, but still unnerving.

Despite the setting—the lights, the rows of babies (oddly quiet), and the din of sounding alarms—the neonatologists and the nursing staff made great efforts to allow my husband and me to be parents. We gave Isabel her first bath, took her temperature and "kangarooed" her for hours at a time. Basically, I would strip Isabel down to her tiny diaper, open my shirt and put her up against my skin—giving her the benefits of my body heat and the familiar rhythm of my heart, which served to regulate her own.

Finally, here was something I could do. But just when we eased into a comfortable rhythm, the alarm on the heart monitor would sound, the lights would flash and a nurse would tell me I had to put Isabel back into her incubator as too many alarms had sounded—I had stimulated her too much. It was a bitter pill. It was largely thanks to my own mother that I was able to keep my frustrations in check—and our situation in perspective. Her visits to the NICU with me were especially moving.

A preemie myself, weighing just six ounces more than Isabel, I had no contact at all with my mother when I was born. It was certainly another era of medicine—and she was allowed to see me only at a distance for the first month of my life. The logic, in those days, was that distance would protect her in the event I died. So, all the bathing and cuddling and rocking and singing I was able to share with my baby were a marvel for my mother. I was glad she was with me to embrace a new generation of medicine and to bond with my baby in a way that wasn't available to her when she became a mother.

I was, nevertheless, completely obsessed with what I perceived as my biggest failure as a mother. I didn't blame myself for my not being able to carry my daughter to term. But I certainly blamed myself for my inability to nurse her. Isabel, like most premature infants, was born with little sucking instinct. So, even after I was given the go-ahead to pump breast milk, it was given to her by way of her feeding tube.

My first couple of efforts at pumping, according to a lactation consultant, produced normal results. But after that, despite regular pumping, doses of fenugreek (an herb some think stimulates breast-milk production), and multiple visits with lactation consultants and La Leche League folks, my production was fast diminishing. Unfortunately, the breastfeeding counselors told me there was no reason why I shouldn't be successful.

Much later I discovered plenty of reasons why I could not nurse: my continued high blood pressure, the medication I was taking and the stress of having an ill child in the NICU. I needed someone (other than my husband) to tell me to stop trying, that my failure to breastfeed was not a measure of my ability to mother. But the way I saw it, I was given only a few opportunities to really help my daughter, and I was a failure at one of the most important. (It didn't help reading comments in an electronic parenting newsletter likening a mother's decision to bottlefeed her baby to putting her into a car without an infant seat.) When I came to my senses and decided to stop the madness, a lactation consultant finally told me that I had plenty of company. It was the rare mother who successfully pumped sufficient milk in such situations.

Despite her medical conditions and the dreaded infant formula, Isabel was growing and getting stronger every day. The nurses tagged her a feeder and a grower. They would dress her up in smocked preemie outfits that were, nevertheless, enormous. They'd glue bows on her head with Karo syrup. "She needs a toy," they said. "She needs tapes of you singing." The nurses were making it clear that Isabel was going home, and she needed to get out of the Similac-issue T-shirts.

Once Isabel tipped the scales at about four pounds, I was finally able to take her home—a month and four days after she was born. I couldn't decide whether I was terrified or ecstatic.

Even though my baby was out of the hospital, my husband and I still had to follow the NICU rules: No visitors under the age of fifteen; visitors who did gain admission to our home had to get sanitized—scrubbing for five minutes up to their elbows; no crowds; and, unfortunately, Isabel was still "wired." She came home equipped with her heart and lung monitor.

Isabel was still experiencing bradycardia and apnea. My husband, mother and I had infant CPR training before Isabel left the hospital, and I posted the CPR guides on our refrigerator door.

The NICU rules were particularly difficult for Isabel's flood of young cousins. They all wanted to see her so badly. I invited them to come over to the house and stand outside the window, and then I held Isabel up to the plate glass so that they could see her. It was like being in the maternity ward at a hospital. It was sort of comical to watch the children making funny faces and oooing and aaahing at Isabel through the window.

Our bouts of parental exhaustion were fierce. During most of Isabel's feedings, her heart rate would drop. She would go limp, and the alarms would sound. Usually the alarms were sufficient to rouse her. The most you ever had to do was thump her on the arm—or sit her up—and her heart rate would normalize. Nights were particularly difficult. The alarms for apnea and/or bradycardia typically sounded several times. After checking on Isabel, we had to record each episode: enter the time, how many beeps and how long it took Isabel to revive. Did she do so on her own? Did we have to intervene? One night, the alarms went off more than sixty times. We were a wreck. Luckily, as Isabel matured, the number of episodes decreased.

Isolation was another problem. As Isabel couldn't go out in "public" until the cold and flu season was officially over, we were confined to the comforts of home until April—six months. Then, Isabel and I ventured out to walk in the neighborhood—with her monitor tucked into the basket under her pram. I did not drive anywhere with her. As most parents know, a car ride is a great way to induce naps. My fears that Isabel would have an episode of bradycardia in the car were sufficient to keep us on our feet.

No sleep coupled with some serious isolation and the constant fretting about Isabel's well-being made for some bleak days. I had a tendency to fixate on the small things rather than the big picture. I remember agonizing over the blisters on Isabel's chest. The monitor's electrodes were glued to her chest, which I had to take off every few days for cleaning, using a solvent to remove the glue. As the electrodes functioned best on particular parts of her chest, Isabel had persistent blisters. I moaned about those far more than I fretted over the apnea.

There were days when I gave in to depression—but a high-needs baby doesn't leave you much space to do so, and it didn't take much imagination to realize how very lucky we were. Weighing less than three pounds at birth, Isabel was still one of the largest babies in the NICU. Many required long-term oxygen via ventilators. Others required surgery. Quite a few of the NICU parents were under twenty years old. I wondered how they were coping. I was very fortunate. I was an adult with a physician at home. How were those other parents coping with the exhaustion? How were they dealing with all the hospital bills? I had met some parents in the NICU whose children were still there. And worse still, I had met a couple of parents whose babies would never leave the hospital.

A freelance writer, I started working again almost immediately. I don't know about the quality of my work at that time, but it provided a great escape. I also spent a lot of time with friends and family who were very supportive. Their love was the fuel I needed to keep going—taking it one day at a time. When Isabel was six months old, she was taken off the heart monitor. In fact, my husband and I insisted she be taken off. Isabel had outgrown the bradycardia. She weighed twelve pounds, and she was developing nicely for a preemie.

Isabel is a normal healthy toddler now, with no long-term medical problems. We are very grateful for that. Of course, my husband and I are a bit shy about having a second child. We always supposed we would have more than one. Even Isabel—with her three-year-old version of biology—insists that I should "grow another baby in my tummy."

My doctor told me that if my husband and I decide to have another baby, there is a good chance, thanks to my age and medical history, that I'd be contending with preeclampsia again. Perhaps it wouldn't be so severe. So, we go on juggling our fears and our visions of family. Along the way, I have discovered the joys of being Isabel's mother. Those joys, coupled with the tricks of a dimming memory, are sometimes more powerful than fears.

Terri's Savvy Strategies

- When things seem bad, use others' perspectives on how it "could be worse." In this way, you can clearly see small bits of light in your own situation.
- Once that positive is identified, focus on it. Look at how you are succeeding in small steps.

The analysis of Terri's experience follows Leisa's story.

My name is Leisa Hart.
I am a fitness expert and the proud mother
of a beautiful baby boy.

Baby's Name: *James Abraham (Abe)*

Date of Birth: *December 29, 2000*

Time of Birth: *2:11 A.M.*

Weight: *7 pounds, 12 ounces*

Length: *20 ½ inches*

My husband Jim and I were so thrilled about taking our baby home from the hospital it was hard for us to contain our excitement. Abe was due on Christmas Eve, but he was born on December twenty-ninth. While Christmas had come and gone, the wonderful feeling of the holiday season still wrapped us in its warm embrace. Jim and I had so much to be thankful for—especially our wonderful, new baby boy.

The morning air was cool the day we took Abe home. The temperature hovered around forty

I was terribly afraid my baby was going to choke.

—LEISA HART

degrees, and the sun was shining. Jim zipped around my hospital room with lightning speed, packing everything in sight. To say Jim was anxious to get us home is an understatement.

After packing my personal belongings, Jim loaded the car and drove everything to the house because we didn't want a lot of stuff in the vehicle when we rode home with Abe. About thirty minutes later, Jim returned to the hospital to get us. As I prepared to leave I discovered he had taken everything home—including my shoes! I couldn't believe it: I was shoeless. All we could do was laugh. I bundled Abe up, cradled him in my arms and walked out of the hospital barefooted and all. Stepping with a confident swagger, I hardly noticed how cold the ground was. The fact that I was a mommy warmed my soul. I felt special, proud and happy—and nothing else mattered.

I climbed into the backseat with Abe for the obvious reason—it's the safest place for a newborn to ride in a car. But I was also afraid he might choke. An incident in the nursery a couple of days earlier had triggered this particular fear. Abe had been lying on his back when I went to visit him in the nursery. All of a sudden, he spit up, started coughing and then started choking. That scared me to death. From that point on, I was terribly afraid my baby was going to choke.

My fear intensified when Jim and I arrived home with Abe. We were not in the house fifteen minutes when I placed my baby in his bassinet, on his back. I put Abe in that position because I had read it was safer for babies to sleep on their backs. Within seconds, however, Abe started choking. Jim was outside. I was alone in the room with Abe, and I panicked. I remember thinking, *Oh my gosh. I just brought him home and he's choking.* I picked up Abe quickly and decided right then and there that I would never put him on his back again. I felt more comfortable with him on his side.

I also took other precautions to make sure my baby wouldn't choke—especially at night while sleeping. I put Abe's bassinet right next to my bed and angled myself to sleep in a position that allowed me to see his face the instant I opened my eyes. I also slept with a nightlight on. I did everything I could think of to make sure my baby would not succumb to choking.

I don't know what fueled my concern. But I do know I was confused because I had read so many conflicting reports when I was pregnant—some of them disturbing—about babies sleeping on their bellies versus babies sleeping on their backs. That confusion, coupled with my witnessing Abe choking in the nursery, played a role in driving my fears.

Jim was very understanding and supportive throughout this trying time, and he helped me cope with the ordeal. He was very attentive to both Abe and me. He pampered me by cooking all our meals, cleaning the house and making sure I took naps whenever Abe went to sleep. If it weren't for Jim's love and compassion, I don't know how I would have gotten over the tremendous fear. It was very unsettling. Sometimes I shudder when I think about it.

Fortunately, that has changed. I don't worry about Abe choking nearly as much and can concentrate even more on being a good mother. Just taking care of Abe makes me feel so much love, the kind of love I have never felt before. My perspective on life has also changed because of my baby. Before Abe was born, I was a workaholic. Being a fitness expert, I was always on the go, working ten- to twelve-hour days. If I wasn't working on my computer, I was teaching exercise classes, shooting videos for my Buns of Steel and Abs of Steel workout tapes or making television appearances to promote them. I would just go, go, go all the time. Jim was constantly telling me, "Slow down. You have to have down time. You've got to relax." But I couldn't.

When I was pregnant my friends used to say, "When you have your baby, your life will change tremendously." I didn't understand what they meant until Abe was born. Since he came along I have learned to slow down. I don't keep such a hectic pace anymore. And I don't run around with never-ending energy. I've learned how to relax—as much as possible with a newborn. Because I now operate in "relax" mode, I think my career is better because my attitude has changed. However, I still have a long list of things to do. But if I only get one of them or none of them done, and I've done a good job taking care of Abe, then that's all that really matters to me.

Leisa's Savvy Strategies

- Learn to relax—it's a great survival skill.
- Believe in yourself and know you can do it if you try.

Letting Go—
The Mother Always Makes It Better Myth

Lori, Leisa and Terri clearly express the major challenge each faced as she assumed the role of mother: letting go. It is the rare mother who avoids this battle; becoming a parent is seldom without costs. Some principle or dream or practice inevitably has to be sacrificed from your former life in favor of your new life with baby. Letting go can come easily. For Terri, Leisa and Lori, however, it often represents a struggle of greater proportions. You may not notice those pieces of your life that have to go when they are small ones or are unimportant to you. But losing more substantial parts of yourself may seem like a never-ending challenge.

Letting Go of "What If"

Terri's first challenge at letting go came with the end to the perfect pregnancy. She had to spend three weeks on bed rest, which she accepted with "relative calm" until told that her baby would be born at twenty-eight-weeks gestation. Terri was able to easily let go of guilt and self-blame about her daughter's premature birth. She knew she could not control the preeclampsia. Many mothers of preemies torment themselves with "what ifs." What if I had exercised more? What if I hadn't missed my prenatal vitamins when I had morning sickness? This kind of thinking fits right in with believing that you have ultimate control: You, as the mother, really could have "made it all right" if only you had made the right choices.

Terri's mother's experience when Terri herself was born prematurely may have helped her handle the surprise of giving birth too soon. She was living proof that preemies could survive. She definitely had to give up on the "perfect baby" myth, however. Her daughter arrived all "red and bony," not pleasingly plump and pink like the baby of magazine advertisements.

Likewise, the myth of "the most wonderful time in your life" flew right out the window with Isabel's birth. There is little that is wonderful about your baby spending time in the NICU, away from her mother, strapped to monitors. Postpartum is not what you expected when you have to stay home for long periods, keep your baby away from others and wheel your baby in her stroller with monitors stowed underneath. Terri had to replace her ideas about bonding through snuggling immediately after birth with the reality of simply touching her daughter's hand.

Controlling What You Can

Although Terri was able to "kangaroo" her daughter for short periods, holding her skin to skin, she had to again compromise. She had to replace her view of what parenting a newborn would be like with the reality of parenting a seriously ill infant. She had to limit contact to decrease stimulation. She probably felt more like a nurse than a mother.

Maggie Redshaw, a member of the psychology faculty at the University of West England, studied the attitudes and experiences of mothers of NICU babies. She found that the separation between mom and baby was perceived as the "worst aspect" of having a premature baby. Terri had to let go of concerns about her daughter's medical problems—the bradycardia and apnea that were a constant in their lives. As these troubles would remind Terri about the fragility of her daughter and her inability to protect her completely, she became fixated on Isabel's blisters from the necessary monitors instead.

This is common when a new mom must face the lack of control she has in one area. She attaches that concern to another issue. Terri could not control Isabel's heart rate or breathing, so she turned her attention to the skin, or surface, problems. She felt she could make those problems better. The illusion of control is comforting, even when the new mom knows that it is just an illusion.

Terri also had to absolve herself from blame about her lack of success at breastfeeding. She made a noble effort at breastfeeding, but it was wearing her out. Terri realized that determination, even though it helps immensely, is not always the deciding factor in breastfeeding success. Certainly her body was under considerable physical and emotional stress, given her medications and blood pressure and Isabel's medical troubles. Once Terri was able to leave the "If I am not a success at breastfeeding, then I am a bad mother" myth behind, she felt better and could focus on other ways to bond with her baby.

Leisa had to relinquish her normal new mom fears. She

feared that Abe would choke. Since this fear was based on several actual events, it was not just fueled by the new mom hormones. The role of oxytocin in enabling mothers to perceive dangers for their babies was discussed in Donna's story. Sometimes these fears are very real, based on the experiences of mom or of baby.

At other times, real concerns are inflated by a new mom's worrisome nature. Many new moms find that gathering more information helps offset these anxieties. You may need to consult with your partner, a doctor or another friend or family member to sort out which fears are real and which are exaggerated. It is also a relief to know that you are doing everything you can to protect your baby from what you fear. Leisa did what she could to guard against her baby's possibility of choking—placing Abe on his side and sleeping where she could see his face.

A New Attitude About Accomplishments

The attitude adjustment that Leisa describes is freeing for her. She had to abandon her previous frantic pace and her focus on immediate outcomes to be a better mother to Abe. Society dictates that the more people accomplish, the more successful they are. Doing more often seems to equal being a "better person." The task of mothering, however, lacks this sense of specific achievement. The day-to-day reality of caring for an infant does not lend itself to a sense of triumph or completion. The milestones come slowly.

The finished product will not be seen for years. It is hard to see how your efforts are paying off when the endless tasks just keep rolling around. You fed the baby, now you need to feed the baby again, and again. There is not much you can cross off your "to do" list. Leisa let go of this pressure by focusing on the item that was always on her list: taking

One trick to help you let go of the torment of "What did I do all day?" is to actually list everything you did for your baby for just one day. You fed the baby (eight times), diapered the baby (twelve times), rocked the baby, changed the baby, cleaned spit-up, kissed the baby, sang to the baby, etc., over and over and over. Keep the list. Post it on the fridge. When you are bemoaning the fact that you got nothing done today, refer back to the list as a way to let go of that drive to see your accomplishments.

care of Abe. She may not have been completing those other tasks on her list. But she knew she was contributing to his well-being, intelligence and success in adulthood by nurturing him now.

You will hopefully see the fruits of your labors in time; just give yourself about twenty-five years. Between now and then, make sure to watch for the clues that the payoff is coming— your child's first word, hug, declaration of love or antics that make you laugh.

Don't belittle the importance of humor. Leisa and her husband demonstrate how laughter is a good coping tool for new parents. When they discovered that she had to walk out of the hospital without her shoes, because he had whisked them home with all the gifts, they were able to laugh. Keeping a sense of humor about the struggles you endure, whether bare feet in December or the fact that your baby just spit up for the

<table>
<tr><td>

Why Humor Is Important

Laughter has been shown to change the chemical makeup of the brain, increasing the flow of "feel good" endorphins—much as in the "runner's high."

- Make time for laughter in your day.
- Watch a comedy show.
- Read the comics.
- Have your partner bring home a joke from work.
- Stop and ponder the humor in a tense moment.

</td></tr>
</table>

thirty-third time today, can make surviving a new baby much more bearable.

Lori came to terms with her fears, and her wish to protect her daughter 110 percent from any discomfort or harm. Her first practice at letting go came in the delivery room. She did not want to even let her husband carry Sarah to her, for fear he would drop her. Lori moved on from there to reality about her food intake and the subsequent effect on her baby.

For the first few days of hospital food, she resolutely refused any item that might upset her baby's tummy. When she slipped and ate the broccoli, she discovered that she had been right to try to guard her baby in this way. There was a cost, to Sarah and Lori, in crying and anguish as they both rode it out as the broccoli passed through the baby's system. But Lori learned through this process that even when parents make a mistake, most of the time it is survivable.

Embrace Your Humanity as a Mother

Becoming a mother means letting go of perfectionist strivings or expectations. You are a human being. Each of the moms telling her story in this book is a human being. Everyone makes mistakes. No one is perfect. Yes, there is tremendous responsibility in parenting your child. Yes, you want to do an excellent job. Excellence is achievable. Perfection is not. You will find yourself facing your imperfections and "slips" into humanity as you parent, just as Lori did when she ate the broccoli.

Remember, babies have been raised by imperfect humans for years. Gandhi's parents were imperfect, so were the parents of Albert Einstein and Mother Teresa. Being human, you cannot always do your best. You will make mistakes and have rotten days. Rather than focusing on the small blunders that are inevitable, move your attention to the "big picture." How often in each day are you succeeding? What are the triumphs or moments to cherish in each day? The women in Weaver and Ussher's study agreed: The positive aspects of motherhood are less tangible than the costs. The things you must let go of, whether life changes or mistakes you make, always seem more obvious than the value added to your life by this small being.

> A nightly count of your small satisfactions about the baby or insights about parenting can greatly outweigh any guilt over small goofs. In the long run, the small goofs will be overshadowed by the triumphs and pleasures.

Coping with Crying

Lori and her husband were challenged to let go when Sarah needed to simply "cry it out." While it is common for partners to disagree on parenting strategies, this issue even has the experts in conflict. There may be as many ideas about whether, when or if to let your baby cry, as there are books on parenting in the library. Psychological research on infancy and crying does offer sound guidance.

- Babies do not understand cause and effect until they are about six months old. This means that you cannot spoil a baby younger than this age by picking him up when he cries.
- Babies cry to communicate something most of the time, and as a parent your job is to figure out what your baby is saying. Sometimes this involves trial and error—rocking, feeding, changing or talking to your baby until he settles down.
- Babies who are carried in slings or front packs through much of the day seem to cry the least of all.
- Babies sometimes get overstimulated and need to cry to reorganize themselves. They cannot talk it through as you might when you are upset about an issue, so they have to cry it out.
- If all your baby's needs are met, you may be able to help your older baby cry less by not responding. Generally, if you have fed, burped, changed, rocked and loved your baby and she refuses to quit crying, brief times in her bed to settle herself down may be helpful.

This idea of overstimulation was addressed in the commentary on Sarah's story and her difficulty in getting her twins to sleep. Sometime between a baby's fifth and seventh month, however, an infant will begin to realize she can control things by crying because she now understands cause and effect. For example, she cries, you show up at her doorway. Your hint that she is just crying to pull you in is the huge smile that engulfs her face when she realizes it worked! Perhaps that is another time to let her cry it out in limited installments, if what she really needs at that point is to go to sleep. To explore this issue further, you may want to read *Touchpoints* by T. Berry Brazelton, M.D., or *Solving Your Child's Sleep Problems* by Richard Ferber, M.D.

The Process of Becoming a Mom

Lori's story illustrates the switch in focus from self to baby. This was seen also in the stories of Andrea (chapter 5) and Annette (chapter 9). Lori began to make this switch with her attention to her diet during pregnancy. Pregnancy gave her a warm-up, emotionally and cognitively, to putting someone else's needs above her own. As Lori's experience makes clear, this is not an absolute transformation once it begins.

It is another example of a process, where the new mother slowly grows into the new habit of thinking of baby first. Two steps forward and one back. This is another human fact. Most growth occurs in this sporadic, slip-sliding pattern. In fact, most habit change requires eighteen months to two years before it takes on automatic status. Give yourself at least that much time to adjust to parenting.

Eleven

Listening—The
Bad Mother Myth

The Bad Mother— Myth or Reality?

Just as society paints a picture of the "good" mother who is perfectly patient, kind and loving, so does the counterpart exist: the "bad" mother. Our culture views mothers within this stark contrast of good or bad. Mothers are either good—with all the perfection expressed above—or just plain bad. There is no middle ground, it seems, within this myth. If you are not "good," then therefore you must be "bad." This certainly is not true. You can make mistakes and still be a good mother.

My name is Myra J.
I'm a radio personality on the nationally
*syndicated **Tom Joyner Morning Show** and*
the proud mother of a beautiful son.

Baby's Name: _Mik-ko_

Date of Birth: _April 11, 1975_

Time of Birth: _11:55 A.M._

Weight: _6 pounds, 11 ounces_

Length: _21 inches_

The very first night I brought my baby home from the hospital I learned a valuable lesson: listen to him. I was living in a cute little townhouse in Normal, Illinois, at the time. One of my neighbors had a cat that liked to climb on my windowsill and whine. The feline was like my very own "Dennis the Menace." The cat made a habit of sitting outside my window wailing every morning at about two or three o'clock and whined so much I couldn't sleep some nights. I tried everything I could think of to keep it away from my window, but it kept coming back.

I felt so guilty because I didn't recognize my baby's voice when he was crying.

—Myra J.

The night I brought Mik-ko home was no exception, or so I thought. I put my baby to sleep in his crib in the nursery, and I went to my room and fell fast asleep. I was deeply asleep when all of a sudden I was awakened like clockwork at about two o'clock in the morning by a whining noise. Totally agitated, I laid in bed for a few minutes cursing the cat under my breath because it was really fraying my nerves. I remember thinking, *Doggone it! Diana's cat is on the windowsill again.* I jumped out of bed quicker than a flash and ran toward my baby's room. I was going to get rid of that cat once and for all. When I got to the nursery, however, it wasn't the cat whining: It was my baby crying. I will never forget how terrible I felt. *Oh my goodness,* I thought. *I am a horrible, horrible mother.*

That was one night I actually wished the cat was whining on the windowsill. I felt so guilty because I didn't recognize my baby's voice. And it never occurred to me that the sound I heard was in fact my baby. Needless to say, that was the one and only time I confused Mik-ko with that cat. Shortly thereafter, my mother hormones kicked in and I was able to distinguish between his cries and figure out what was wrong when he was crying: whether he was wet, hungry or sleepy. Of course, there were times when I didn't have all of the answers, but I never gave up trying to figure things out.

One day, my husband and I left Mik-ko with one of my girlfriends while we went to a movie. When we returned home my baby was screaming at the top of his lungs. It was one of those cries that sends chills up and down your spine. Frantic, I ran to Mik-ko and asked my girlfriend what was wrong. She told me my baby had been hungry and she had given him evaporated milk—because he had drunk all the breast milk I had left for him. Mik-ko had never had evaporated milk before. What was worse, he couldn't digest it. My baby was throwing up all over the place.

I felt so guilty. It was like one of those times when you know you should be doing a better job of watching your child, but you're not. Then he falls down and skins a knee and he screams in pain and you feel worse than he does. I felt awful. All I could do was apologize to my baby for not leaving enough breast milk at home for him to drink. It was as if I were saying, *I'm sorry I took the food with me. I should have left a breast at home for you. I'm so sorry. Please forgive me.*

One thing about listening that will make you feel like you're losing your mind is this: You will think every baby sounds like your baby. I remember I left Mik-ko at home with my husband while I went to the mall. When I got there I heard a baby crying. I knew I had left Mik-ko at home, but I could have sworn I heard him crying in the mall. I kept looking around expecting to see him. The funny thing about that is it never seems to end. It feels like you are constantly hearing your baby's voice—as if his spirit is always with you. For example, when Mik-ko was about two and a half, I left him home with his father while I ran errands. While I was shopping, I heard a toddler yelling, "Mommy!" Instinctively, I turned around and answered, "Yes, baby." Of course the little boy looked at me with a puzzled expression on his face as if to say, "You're not my mommy." And I stood frozen in place thinking, *You're not my son.*

As Mik-ko got older and started talking more, I also learned the importance of letting him know what he was saying was important, that he could always talk to me no matter what. I've learned over the years that there is no greater love than that between a mother and child. It is totally unconditional. And the bottom line is children are the greatest blessing you will ever have. If you learn to listen to them, that blessing will be even sweeter.

Myra's Savvy Strategies

• Put aside preconceived notions about what your child is communicating and really listen to him.

• Know that you can make mistakes and not be a horrible mother!

Analysis of Myra's story follows Lisa's story. Lisa's story explores more about how listening is important between mother and baby.

My name is Lisa Rayam.
I'm a television news anchor and the proud mother
of a beautiful little boy.

Baby's Name: _Jordan_

Date of Birth: _April 9, 1999_

Time of Birth: _11:21 A.M._

Weight: _8 pounds, 14 ounces_

Length: _21 inches_

I will never forget the day my baby got his first ear infection. That pain-filled night is deeply embedded in my memory. In fact, I still get chills when I think about hearing my baby's piercing cry. Jordan was only two months old. I had put him to bed without incident. However, a couple of hours later his hair-raising screams cut through the darkness and my heart. My husband and I jumped out of bed at about the same time and ran quickly to the nursery. We found Jordan lying in his crib, sweating profusely and wailing because of excruciating pain.

On those nights when Jordan was crying and I didn't know why, it just hurt me and I would start crying, too.

—LISA RAYAM

Needless to say, I panicked. What mother wouldn't? I grabbed my baby as fast as I could, held him in my arms and asked him repeatedly, "What's wrong?" Lord knows I was praying he could answer. Stress lines creased my husband's forehead as we tried to figure out what was causing our baby so much discomfort. It was puzzling because during the day Jordan was fine. He nursed well and slept like normal.

I knew something was seriously wrong, but I didn't know what ailment had stricken my baby. Nervous, I held Jordan in my arms and paced the floor like a lioness protecting her cub. My mind was racing as tears streamed down my face. I was trying to piece together the day's events in an effort to pinpoint the source of Jordan's pain. Like a snap, I remembered I had a medical guidebook for infants. I grabbed it, flipped through the pages quickly, found a section on ear infections, read the symptoms and figured that was the culprit. My husband and I rushed Jordan to the hospital. Sure enough he was diagnosed with an ear infection. Jordan kept getting them until he was about five months old. That was terrifying because I was breastfeeding him at the time, and my doctor told me breastfeeding made babies healthy. Jordan, however, kept getting sick.

Stinging with guilt, I started blaming myself. I thought, *Maybe I'm nursing him lying down too much and fluid is building up in his ears. Or maybe I'm not recognizing the onset soon enough before the infection settles in.* I became paranoid. I started double-checking everything: making sure Jordan's head was covered, his feet were covered, that he was warm—but nothing seemed to work. That really took its toll after awhile. I hated with a passion to see my baby sick and in pain. I began to ride myself and started to question whether I was attentive enough.

The guilt was overwhelming. It got to the point that whenever Jordan cried hysterically I thought he had an ear infection. Nine out of ten times he didn't. On those nights when Jordan was crying and I didn't know why, it just hurt me and I would start crying, too. Every little thing was nerve-wracking after that. I started relying on "mother's wisdom." I began calling my mom, my mother-in-law and my sister-in-law and asking, "What do I do for this?" "What do I do for that?" It didn't take long to discover everyone had a different remedy for everything.

When Jordan had an ear infection I was told, "He should be wearing shoes," or "He should be wearing socks," or "You need to cover his head." My husband and I were inundated with so much information it sent us into a tizzy. When we were at our wits' end we started taking sides. It was like being members of opposing debate teams. I would say, "Well, my mom said do this." And he would say, "My mom said do that." That created a lot of pressure because I wanted to do things a certain way because my mom told me to. And my husband wanted to do things a certain way because of suggestions he received from his family.

At one point, I was getting advice from my husband's mother, his father, his sister, my mother and my father, and it was too much. While I love my family members dearly and respect their advice, the input was overwhelming and the pressure was overbearing. Instead of sitting down and saying, "Honey, how should we handle this?" or "This is what the doctor said," or "This is what I read, what do you think?" my husband and I were listening to a wealth of people with a wealth of conflicting information. That caused us to get on each other's backs.

My husband and I finally sat down one day and looked at each other and realized we had to find peace and harmony. After careful consideration, we decided not to solicit too much help from other people. We made a concerted effort to listen to Jordan's doctor, read books and rely on our own instincts. When we started implementing that plan I became a lot more comfortable as a mother.

There were still times when I felt lost and helpless. When answers were beyond my reach I would rush Jordan to his pediatrician. In fact, I think during his first two months, my husband and I took him to the doctor a zillion times for every little symptom. Thank goodness his doctor was patient and understood I was only trying to protect my baby and make sure he was safe.

The whole situation was so mentally taxing, but I finally realized I am human. I will make mistakes. That does not mean I am not a good mother. And while advice from Mom, Grandma and others is good, too much advice can be just that—too much! I feel more comfortable now being a mother because my husband and I decided to make our own decisions and trust our instincts. That helped me build my self-confidence, and I'm very comfortable now in my role as mother.

Lisa's Savvy Strategies

- When asking for advice from others, use that input for information to aid your decision, not as the "final answer."
- Trust your own inner wisdom about your baby and what works for your life.

Listening—Resisting the "Bad" Mother Myth

Lisa and Myra are wise women: Each has identified an invaluable tool in mothering effectively. That tool, of course, is listening. Every mother has this intrinsic ability, which goes beyond simply hearing the tone of your baby's cry or the simple face value of the words uttered. The depth of listening required to be an effective mother involves multiple levels and really knowing your child. You have to understand not only your child's pronunciation or tones. You have to read meaning beyond the words in the context of who this particular child is. What Myra and Lisa refer to here is the same as what mothers in Stephanie Brown, Rhonda Small and Judith Lumley's study recognized as part of being a good mother. That is spending time with your children so you can comprehend their needs and guide them according to those needs.

Since this knowledge only comes with watching, studying and immersing yourself in the world of your child, of course it is again not an absolute or instantly gained. It is simply one more part of the process in becoming a "good enough" mother. You have to grow to know your child and her needs. If you pay attention to what you are learning, your skills in this regard will develop along with your child.

Myra and Lisa both grew into the role. Each was critical of herself because she could not read her child's needs or cries right away. In line with societal mother myths, each woman expected to be perfect. If not perfect, then the alternative to perfect was "horrible mother." Lisa and Myra both moved past that initial confusion stage and became adept at figuring out what would help their child's problems. They also grew to be less self-critical, repeating themes explored in the stories of

> **Tips to Remember on the Way to "Good Enough" Mothering**
>
> Good mothers make mistakes. This does not cancel out their good qualities.
>
> Mothers cannot always protect their children completely from pain and suffering.

Donna, Shirley and Sarah. They realized that there are few truly bad mothers. Instead, they learned to keep realistic expectations in mind.

Learning to Listen

As a mother, how can you put listening skills to work?

- First of all, you must tune in to your child. Be present in the moment with your child whenever you are with your child.

- Turn off those other worries and concerns, at least for awhile. Write them down if that helps you to put them aside for the moment.

- You may have to take a deep breath and say to yourself: time for baby. With a newborn, this may mean simply studying or watching your baby when she is awake and quiet. Look at her, see how she looks around and takes in her world.

- When she begins to gurgle and coo, listen so you can imitate her. Cooing back will help her develop speech. You will have to focus on the sounds she is making in order to do this.
- With a child who is beginning to speak, resist the urge to jump in and assume what your child is saying. Let her finish, do not cut her off or complete her sentences for her. This may at times mean biting your tongue if you are hurried and want the words to come out now so you can move on.
- When your child is a bit older, preschool age perhaps, make sure you arrange time in your day for listening to her without distractions. The ride home from day care or sitting on her bed at night works well.

Certainly you cannot sit down and turn your full attention to your child for huge chunks of each day. You have other responsibilities and relationships to balance. Besides, children do need to learn that they share their world with others, taking turns not only at being the center of the universe but in listening as well. Otherwise, they will monopolize kindergarten "circle time." But keep an ear tuned to what your child is saying throughout your day. Children communicate not just in words but with whining, foot stomping or hugging. You will learn to "kick in" to full attention when necessary.

Focus on Your Child's Uniqueness

Keep in mind that this child is not you and may have different motivations, preferences or opinions than you. You will not realize these unique aspects of your child if you enter the relationship convinced that he is "just like me" or "his father reincarnated." You must figure out his individual needs and quirks. Remember, listening is not just for your benefit, so you can learn about your child. It is also for the child's benefit. Offer feedback to your child. This does not mean solving the child's problems, this means reflecting back his feelings, helping him identify what he is feeling and validating those feelings. It means saying, "Of course you are sad (or excited, or angry)—that would make me sad too." This is how children learn to understand and trust their feelings, to know that it is okay to feel a certain way.

When they can identify feelings in that way, children can use feelings as guides. This is part of becoming emotionally healthy adults. For an excellent guide in learning listening skills and understanding your baby, look at *Dear Parent* by Magda Gerber, *Your Self-Confident Baby* by Magda Gerber and Allison Johnson, or *Why Is My Baby Crying?* by Bruce Taubman, M.D. Check out *How to*

Listening Skills— A Quick Guide

Turn off your thoughts.

Really hear the words your child is saying.

State the feelings back to your child and identify them—for example, "You sound mad."

Offer a course of action, or ask your child, "What do you think you should do?"

Talk So Kids Will Listen and Listen So Kids Will Talk by Adele
Faber and Elaine Mazlish for older children.

Phantom Crying and Other Oddities

Myra had to wade through the fog of sleep deprivation and
new motherhood to begin to figure out her baby's cries and
act like a mother, just as Annette had to make that transition
to thinking like a mother. When Myra thought her baby was a
cat, she was probably still exhausted from the birth and still
thinking like a childless person. Once she turned her "listening" ability on, she found it hard to let go.

Everywhere she turned, it seemed her baby was crying or
calling out. The female hormones, particularly those involved
in breastfeeding, are thought to enhance this ability. This may
be why the new mother hears the baby crying to be fed in the
night while dad saws logs. Some women even report "phan-
tom crying." The new mom thinks she hears her baby crying
even when the house is silent.

While hormones help to "turn on" this skill, over time it
simply becomes a habit that is hard to turn off. This can
explain what often happens in a group of small children and
mothers. One child cries "Mom!" and four or five women
answer. They are simply programmed to do so, having to
respond in this way day in and day out. This is what Myra did
when she encountered the small boy calling for his mother on
her shopping trip one day. Women in the study by Jane
Weaver and Jane Ussher reported this, too. Sensitivity to other
children's troubles became great. Many new mothers find

they cannot stay tuned to news events after they have children. Any reports of harm to children, be it illness or injury, just seem to hurt too much because of this increase in sensitivity.

A Heartfelt Connection

Myra felt that this habit of always listening represented another facet of her relationship with Mik-ko. It seemed to her that his spirit was always with her. This happens when mothers are so deeply connected to their children that they feel that connection in every moment.

This is true for many mothers. In fact, you may feel like your child still resides within you, just as he did during pregnancy, even when you are physically apart. Your hearts are still linked in some way. This is a reflection of the psychological attachment that is explored in greater depth in Amanda Davis's story in chapter 13. Not only do you stay so intensely connected in a spiritual manner to your child, but you can feel disappointed when pieces of the distinctness between you and your child become more obvious. But you love him no matter what—even when he follows his own path. That is what the parent-child bond means. It is accepting that this baby is a human being in his own right, one who will always be loved by the parent because of the similarities and the differences between parent and child.

Sorting Through Competing Advice

Lisa's story points out the difficulty in listening to multiple sources of advice. Contradictory advice even began to cause conflict in the couple. Most couples go through this stage as they try to sort out how they will be the best parents they can. It is natural to gather information from all sources you trust—family and friends and experts. Quite naturally, these sources usually have varying ideas of what is "right," and often this sends the new parents right into deep conflict, as it did with Lisa and her husband. When a couple marries and is establishing a home together the task at hand is to sort out "how to do things." Each person brings ideas from the family in which they were raised, plus any preferences each has developed on their own. Even when couples are not aware of it, they are each working to define their life together according to their own family agenda.

When a baby arrives, couples continue hashing out the "family agenda." Will they be low-key, like his parents—or constantly involved, like her parents? Is his mom right, or is her mom right? Can she make decisions about money and about whether she will stay home full time with the baby, or will he make the decisions? All decisions that have to be made have the potential for conflict. Over time, the couple must do just what Lisa and her husband did.

- They listened to each other to begin to identify and solve the problem.
- They talked it out. They collected all the information as background, not as a final judgment.
- They decided to focus on their instincts and Jordan's doctor's opinions.
- They tried to stick to their decisions—together.

In the stories of Kimberly and Angela, parents were urged to devise a mission statement to guide their parenting. The process of decision making was explored in chapter 7. You may wish to refer back to those guidelines. Ideally, the couple can embark on any decision making task together, so they will have a mutually defined focus and goal that can be used to settle disputes.

They might read various opinions in books and report back to each other. Then they can try to find the commonalties in the diverse information they have collected. That means putting aside opinions and really listening to what a partner is reporting. It means listening to a partner's feelings, too, and valuing them. In Lori's story, her husband wanted her to let the baby "cry it out." Even though he may have had expert advice backing that strategy, Lori simply could not do it. It did not "feel right" to her. She felt like she was abandoning her baby at a time of need. Couples need to learn to respect those feelings in each other and use, rather than dismiss, them when making decisions together.

Twelve

Mothering Solo—The Perfect Little Families Myth

Perfect Little Families— Myth or Reality?

Cultural images are powerful in creating this myth. Most women believe they will enter motherhood fulfilling the 1960's television sitcom ideal of mom, dad, 2.3 kids and a dog. The "perfect little family" seems like the only way to embark upon this life change. But the reality is that as many as one-third of babies are born to single mothers. Many more families contend with work demands which leave parents feeling like they are on their own.

My name is Rosaura Aburto McDonough.
I am a financial analyst and the proud mother
of a beautiful baby girl.

Baby's Name: *Annalise*

Date of Birth: *June 26, 2001*

Time of Birth: *8:33 P.M.*

Weight: *6 pounds, 6 ounces*

Length: *20 inches*

There is nothing worse than wanting something you can't have. I mean really longing, hoping and praying for something as precious as a baby—and at the same time knowing there is a strong possibility you will never have one. Never experience the miracle of life. That is very disheartening. My husband and I tried for more than two years to have a baby without success. That may not seem like a long time to you, but to me it seemed like an eternity.

We visited doctor after doctor and tried several different fertility drugs, but nothing worked. Disappointment settled in with lightning speed. As hard as it was to do, I

I was worried about my husband missing out on watching our little one grow up.

—Rosaura Aburto McDonough

accepted the fact that I was never going to get pregnant. I was never going to carry a baby. I was never going to feel life growing inside of me. That had a profound affect on me and left me puzzled. I couldn't understand why I was being denied the one thing I wanted more than anything in the world. Thorough medical exams didn't reveal anything physically wrong with me or my husband. Yet I could not conceive.

Determined to satisfy our desire to have a baby, my husband and I looked into adopting a child. We were terribly excited. After careful consideration, we decided to move forward with the process because we knew we could give a baby a lot of love and a warm nurturing home. We started investigating adoption agencies and preparing ourselves to become adoptive parents. I was thrilled about the prospects of becoming an adoptive mom.

In the midst of our search, it occurred to me that I had missed my period. I didn't invest a lot of time worrying about it. I figured my cycle was off track because of the fertility drugs I was taking—that happened occasionally. Still, motivated by the slight chance that I could be pregnant, I took five home pregnancy tests. Yes, five! Every single one came back negative. A wave of sadness fell over me.

Curious to find out what was wrong with my body I called my doctor and shared what happened. She scheduled an appointment. When I went to see her she gave me a thorough examination, a blood test and encouraged me to take it easy. "Relax. Don't worry," she said. It was hard not to. The following day, I was sitting at my desk in my office when the telephone rang. I picked it up and my doctor announced, "Rosy, I just want you to know you are very, very, very pregnant." I couldn't believe it. My prayers had been answered.

"I'm going to have a baby," I mumbled to myself. I was so happy I couldn't think about anything else for the rest of the day. My lips curled into a huge smile I couldn't get rid of no matter how hard I tried. I even walked into a couple of tense, high-powered meetings with this pleasant expression on my face that puzzled my esteemed colleagues.

My husband was in Phoenix, Arizona, when I learned the wonderful news. He had gone there to attend a friend's wedding.

I didn't want to just come out and tell him about the baby on the telephone. Instead, I wanted to send him a very special message across the miles. I carefully wrapped up a cute white baby outfit, a bow and a pair of booties in a nice gift box and sent it FedEx. Then I waited to hear from my husband. Puzzled, he phoned me immediately after opening the package. "What is this?" he asked. "Honey, we're going to have a baby," was all I managed to say.

To say my husband was surprised would be an understatement. I gave him all of the details, and he couldn't believe his ears. Talking faster than an auctioneer at an estate sale, my husband told me he was going to change his flight, skip the wedding and come home. I assured him I was fine, and we could celebrate after he returned home from the ceremony. It was hard, but my husband calmed down. We both looked forward to a romantic dinner and movie, in honor of our baby.

"What a miracle!" When I first saw my little girl I couldn't believe my eyes. All the time I spent hoping and praying for her and taking medical treatments was worth it. Annalise was absolutely beautiful. I couldn't hold her at first because I was in a lot of pain following a C-section. A nurse was kind enough to bring my little miracle close to me so that I could see her sweet face. I was glad to meet my baby, but terribly disappointed because I could not hold her.

When I was carrying Annalise inside, I imagined giving birth to her and the doctor placing her on my chest. I would be the first person she saw, smelled and grasped. When that didn't happen, coupled with the fact that I couldn't even hold her, I was deeply saddened. However, about eight hours later my spirits were lifted. I was physically able to embrace my baby. She was so beautiful. It felt absolutely wonderful to feel her little body next to mine.

My husband and I could not have been happier—especially when we took our daughter home. Annalise was such a good baby. She brought us so much joy. While I was tired and couldn't sleep, I still felt happy. I was worried, however, about my husband missing out on watching our little one grow up. A software salesman, my husband was on the road a lot. He traveled to Canada and to Europe. That kept him away from home at least five days a week.

I realized my husband had to work, but I felt extremely sad because he was not home to witness the little things our baby was doing—like smiling in her sleep. I wish he could have seen her face the first time she did that. Or see how she liked to be wrapped and rocked. They were little things that seemed huge to me, and I hated the fact that my husband didn't have an opportunity to share the same special moments. I knew he wanted to be home instead of jumping on planes. I knew he loved me and our daughter. I knew he wanted to be with us, but he just couldn't. That really hurt.

I didn't think my husband's traveling would bother me so much before Annalise was born. However, when she arrived it did. When he was home, and I saw how much he loved her and cared for her, I felt even worse. My husband was the perfect daddy. He changed Annalise, put her to sleep and would even get her so that I could feed her. He was very comfortable with our daughter. It tore him apart every time he had to leave us.

My husband tried very hard to change his schedule so that he wouldn't have to travel so frequently and could spend more time with me and our baby. Annalise is such a miracle. We are so grateful to have her. I have come to the realization that God sometimes sends you things because you deserve them and you work hard for them. I took comfort knowing one day my husband would be able to share more special moments with us. As it turned out, he got a new job that doesn't require any traveling. Now, he spends a lot of time with Annalise and me—and rarely misses a special moment.

Rosaura's Savvy Strategies

- Focus on the blessings: her husband loved her and the baby, and he did not choose to travel.
- Persist in changing an unfavorable situation.

Analysis of Rosaura's story follows Kalani's story. Kalani is a young mother who also dealt with mothering without a partner.

My name is Kalani Patterson.
I am a college student and the proud
mother of a beautiful little boy.

Baby's Name: *Jaelin*

Date of Birth: *June 22, 2000*

Time of Birth: *9:17 A.M.*

Weight: *6 pounds, 1 ounce*

Length: *18 1/4 inches*

The day I found out I was pregnant I felt as if all my hopes and dreams were shattered. I was an eighteen-year-old high school senior looking forward to going to college. Sitting in an examining room, I waited with my mother for my doctor to return with the results of various tests. The door to the tiny room creaked when it opened. My doctor paused just long enough for his body to fill its frame. Then he walked into the room and sat on his blue, leather, rolling stool. My doctor looked into my mother's eyes and in a calm steady

> When I first brought Jaelin home I was depressed—I kept thinking I can't do anything now.
>
> —KALANI PATTERSON

voice told her I was four and half months pregnant. Pregnant! Stunned, I didn't hear anything he said after that.

Disappointed, my mother didn't say a word. She merely stood up and walked out of the room. At that moment I felt like my freedom walked out with her. In a daze, I got up from the examining table and walked over to a nearby window and stared at the busy street below. There was a lot of traffic and people were coming and going, but I didn't see anyone or anything in particular. I was just looking and thinking, *I can't believe this.* I had never been so shocked before in my life.

For a while, I was angry with myself for getting pregnant because that meant I wasn't going away to college in the fall—if ever. I had let my parents and myself down, and I had tremendous challenges ahead of me. It was clear I had made a big mistake. While my parents were upset, they told me they loved me, told me everything was going to be all right, and told me they would support me—but I had to finish high school and college.

I was in my last year of high school, and I was having a baby. When my girlfriends noticed my body transforming— my face, breasts, legs and arms were getting fat—they teased me about gaining weight. When I told them I was pregnant, half of them ended our friendship. The other half continued to be friends with me. I needed my friends' support more than ever, especially since my boyfriend broke up with me after I told him I was carrying his child. At first he said, "I'll take care of you and our baby." He later claimed he was not the father of our child and stopped coming around. That hurt me terribly, but I wasn't going to let my broken heart stop me from accomplishing my immediate goal of graduating from high school.

Things got really tough the more I developed in my pregnancy. I was tired and hungry all the time, my stomach was getting bigger, my ankles were swollen. I was falling behind in my classes, and I was thinking about quitting school. One day I told my girlfriends I didn't think I could finish. I didn't believe I could carry my baby and keep up the hectic pace. It was too much. My friends told me I could make it through high school and college if I concentrated on my work. I found it hard to believe them. I had heard that when most girls get pregnant in high school they don't do anything with their lives. I didn't want to be like that.

I went home after school that day and wrote down how I felt about being pregnant on a sheet of notebook paper, and how I wanted to make it through high school and college. I was so upset I called my grandmother and shared my feelings. She was very understanding. My grandmother made me feel better when she told me stories about how she felt when she had her first baby.

I took comfort in her words—especially when she told me I could finish high school and college—but I had to work very hard and apply myself. I went back to school the next day with a renewed faith. Every day my friends encouraged me saying, "You can make it." Their support and my will to succeed helped get me through each day. Before I knew it, it was time for graduation, and I was getting my high school diploma.

I was happy I graduated, but that was only the beginning of my long educational journey. I was accepted at a local community college and registered to study computer science. Determined to graduate and get a good job, I worked hard. I wanted to be able to take care of my baby who was born a few weeks before classes started.

I didn't know labor would be so intense. It was very painful. However, when the doctor placed my baby boy on my stomach the miracle of birth dulled my memory of the pain. I focused on how beautiful my son, Jaelin, was. He was so tiny. I couldn't believe how small he was.

When I first brought Jaelin home I was depressed. I kept

thinking, *I can't do anything now.* I wasn't going away to college, and I thought I was missing out on things with my girlfriends. All of my dreams seemed to have crumbled into a million pieces. Not only that, I was afraid to hold my baby. I didn't know how. I would only hold Jaelin if I was sitting and my mother was in the room helping me. My fears were heightened because my baby seemed to cry all the time. I would get angry and give him to my mother. I couldn't handle it.

I was nervous, tired and cranky—all the time. I had severe mood swings that changed like the weather. I kept thinking, *If only I hadn't gotten pregnant.* I was afraid of mothering because I didn't know how to care for my newborn baby— and to be honest, I didn't want the responsibility. My mother taught me everything, from how to bathe Jaelin to how to dress and undress him. She was great, but I knew I couldn't depend on her forever. When I finally started getting the hang of caring for my baby I kept telling myself: *You can do this. This is your baby. You're not going to hurt him.* I kept repeating that over and over to myself until I developed confidence.

While my mother was there for me and was a big help, I realized Jaelin was my responsibility and I had to take care of him. There were times when it seemed like as soon as I cleared one hurdle another one popped up. Stressed nearly to the max, I had to reach deep inside myself for strength to forge ahead. Before classes started at the community college I had to find a babysitter. It was hard, but I was lucky enough to have a family friend who agreed to care for Jaelin while I was in school. That was comforting because I knew he would be safe.

Developing a routine for Jaelin and me was another big challenge. I got up every morning around eight, got ready for class, got Jaelin up, dressed and fed him, took him to the babysitter and then I went to school. I had classes from ten until two, worked from three until eight, three days a week, took care of Jaelin and did homework. I rarely had time to spend by myself or with my girlfriends. The few times I saw them, they would ask me all kinds of questions—including some that were sexual in nature. I told my friends to practice abstinence and not make the same mistake I had.

While it is very hard being a teenage mother, I love my baby more than anything in the world. Sometimes I find myself looking at Jaelin, and I just melt. He brings me so much joy. That motivates me to stay on track and work feverishly to accomplish my goals. I have to, for Jaelin's sake, and for mine.

Kalani's Savvy Strategies

- Use writing or journaling to vent feelings and keep some perspective in your life.
- Talk to yourself in a kind and encouraging voice.

Mothering Solo—
The Perfect Little Families Myth

Becoming a mother is one of the hardest challenges most women face, as we have seen in the previous stories, because of the magnitude and breadth of the changes. Women have to weather change in all of their relationships—with friends, family and spouse. They change the way they view themselves. They alter how their lives are structured and how they think.

Rosaura and Kalani added another dimension to that difficult transition. They were mothering their babies alone. It is clear that single parents like Kalani and women whose partners travel frequently like Rosaura have less social support, less chance for relief. The nonstop nature of infant care, being on duty seven days a week for twenty-four hours a day, is exhausting, even when sharing the load with a partner. The lack of breaks on a consistent basis can lead the new mother to greater exhaustion and discouragement.

The incredible responsibility of mothering a newborn is another element that is distinctly different for new mothers who are functioning practically solo. The single mother not only has to make decisions day in and day out on her own. She may have no one she can use as a sounding board, no one for whom this baby is so important. It can be terrifying for a mother operating largely on her own to imagine her own vulnerability. What if she is ill? Who will care for the baby? Who will keep them clothed and fed? All this adds up to a considerable increase in stress for a mother on her own.

Grieving the Loss of the Ideal

Many women who are mothering alone find themselves grieving the loss of the "ideal little family." Women truly want to achieve this myth, the two parents and baby together. But they need to remember that they can still be wonderful parents and have a fulfilling sense of family—even if their circumstances don't match the ideal.

Because their life does not fit the family model the new mother may have always envisioned, her disappointment and grief are real. Rosaura is open with her sadness about her husband's travelling. Before the baby was born, she did not mind his travel and did not anticipate that it would bother her. But their joy together at Annalise's arrival only made her miss him more. She wanted so badly for them to be a family together. Every event that he missed was another stab of pain for her. It is never easy to have one partner gone frequently. The couple cannot support each other on baby care. They miss each other and miss their growing sense of family.

Infertility and Expectations

For Rosaura and her husband, the fact that Annalise was a "miracle baby" made being apart even harder. Research has shown that women who have invested years of energy and expense in fertility treatments have higher expectations than usual for the postpartum period being "the most wonderful time of their life." They have worked so long to have a baby, and perhaps spent their life savings, that they truly believe everything will be perfect. The infertility may have also explained why she found it so hard to wait to hold her baby after birth. She had already been waiting longer than she liked for this event in her life.

Finally getting the baby you want means you now have everything you ever hoped for. How could you not be happy? Since expectations are higher than for other new mothers, the impact of reality may be greater. This is likely what happened with Rosaura and her husband. She really wanted the "perfect family" so badly. It was difficult to tolerate any deviation from that ideal picture. The fact that her husband was such a devoted dad hurt even more. She was telling herself their life together could really be flawless, if only he were not traveling.

Mothers who become parents after infertility need to guard themselves against such high hopes. Of course you will be happy to finally reach this goal you have been striving for. But you will still be the same person you were before, as will your partner. You will continue to grapple with the same doubts, frustrations and conflicts in your life.

In Rosaura's story, she demonstrates that the few aspects you dislike in your life aren't necessarily cast in stone. Her husband worked hard at finding a new job, and he finally found one that did not require extensive travel. Apply the same strategy to your other disappointments, and you will be able to solve those problems as well—and enjoy your baby.

Coping with a Travel Schedule

When one partner travels extensively, the family often has a more difficult period of adjustment before they genuinely feel like a family. Rosaura does not speak of this, but it is a common problem. If the new mother is at home, she certainly finds her niche. She is functioning on her own caring for the baby between her partner's brief sojourns at home. She becomes so accustomed to "doing it all" that it seems complicated to let him back into the family circle when he is home.

She may view her partner as an interloper. He suddenly appears ready to go full throttle with the baby when he does not know the routine. He tries to do it his way rather than use successful methods the new mom has devised. With his different style he may even alienate the baby who has not seen him much. Consequently, the baby cries at the sight of him. On the other hand, since he is gone often, he may have no confidence in helping and so do little to help—increasing the new mother's resentment that she is the sole functioning parent. He is not sure how to fit in. She is not sure how to help him relax with the baby, or vice versa.

All around, this makes for an unpleasant scenario, and for tense weekend after tense weekend. Many couples that must cope with the travel schedule of either parent find that structure can provide relief from these woes. When the traveling partner first returns, family time with both parents and baby is the best idea. This eases the adjustment for the baby and lets the absent parent be "briefed" by the at-home parent. Over the course of the traveling parent's time at home, it often works well to allow the at-home parent to take a break from baby care while the other parent stays "on duty" with the baby.

Allowing the traveling parent to take a rest break as well, together with setting aside private time as a couple, are also important parts of the weekend scenario. When you allow for both "together" and "apart" time, you can achieve a balance between the needs of the parents as a couple, the needs of the baby to relate to the absent parent, and the needs of each parent to have some personal time to recharge before the next round of baby care and travelling begins.

A Universal Loss for Single Parents

Kalani's grief at possibly postponing her college plans delineates another way in which women parenting alone may grieve the "perfect little family" myth. She was very disheartened to be pregnant at eighteen, and to have the baby's father refuse to take responsibility. Almost every woman who has a baby alone goes through this loss. Few women envision being a single parent when they imagine themselves as mothers. The picture routinely includes a complete, balanced family, not a lopsided one with one parent. Not only was Kalani mourning the loss of this ideal, she had significant holes in her life as a result of this baby. She lost friends; she lost the relationship with the baby's father; she had to change her college plans and feared she would lose that dream.

The Dual Crisis of Adolescent Motherhood

Kalani's entry into motherhood was a double whammy. She had the developmental crisis of becoming a mother heaped on top of the developmental crisis of adolescence. Both crises involve incredible changes in self—physically, emotionally, socially—and thus represent overwhelming stress. Motherhood forced Kalani to switch her focus away from herself and her goals to her son. This was at a time when she should have been a self-centered adolescent.

Kalani's discouragement was understandable. She did well to focus her anger at her situation, rather than at her baby. She was not mad at Jaelin. She was mad at losing her dreams and having her life restricted in this way. Many new mothers are surprised by the anger they feel at the baby. When they can step back and realize it is not the baby they are angry at, but the changes in their life, then they can take appropriate steps to address the anger in a healthy way.

Steps in Addressing Anger:

- Problem solving is the first step in facing anger. Focus on what might improve your day-to-day life, then work to make that change a reality.
- Exercise can be extremely useful in working out angry feelings that seem to persist for no reason. Aerobic exercise appears to burn up angry feelings very effectively.
- Some women find it useful to express anger symbolically, by pounding on the bed with a plastic bat or tearing up old phone books. These activities are best done in timed

segments. That way, the new mother may not feel like the anger will take over.

- Follow any physical expressions of anger with some calming, relaxing time for self—soaking in the tub or talking to a trusted friend.
- After the anger is relieved, the new mother can review the positive aspects of her life.

Kalani conquered these multiple challenges by employing tools that can ease the adjustment for any new mother. She had a good support system in her family. While her parents were disappointed, they gave her financial support as long as she would stay in school. Her grandmother offered her emotional support, talking with Kalani about her own experience in becoming a parent and validating Kalani's normal fears.

Kalani also had encouragement from friends, urging her to believe in herself and stay in school. In addition, she had a trusted family friend provide day care for Jaelin. This kind of practical support is important to decrease a mother's fears about leaving a new baby. All her sources of social support may have made the difference in reaching her goals. Support like this is critical for any new mother, but can be the ballast that tips the scales in her favor when a woman is parenting solo.

Writing It Out

Kalani wrote out her feelings at one of her darkest moments, focusing on her desire to be able to make it through her education. The power of journaling in this manner has been well-documented by research. Individuals who write out feelings and goals not only move through negative feelings more quickly, they are more likely to achieve their goals. Journaling in this manner does not have to be wonderful prose, or placed in a lovely keepsake book, or even done according to a schedule. Many new moms use this as a tool when feelings are about to overwhelm them.

> ## A Quick Guide to Journaling
>
> - Use your journal to simply vent and clear out angry feelings.
> - Don't worry about flowery prose or proper grammar.
> - Just put your raw emotions down on paper and then leave them alone for a time.
> - After venting, you may want to tear up your writing and throw it away—or simply symbolically close the book and leave your "bad" feelings behind until the next time.

The Importance of Structure

Structure and routine in her life helped Kalani manage her time and move forward as well. This principle is important for all new moms. Having a schedule, as much as the baby permits, often makes the new mother feel in control of her life again, rather than feeling like her life controls her. Flexible structure is the goal with a tiny baby. Set simple goals, such as, "I will take a walk every morning, sometime between 9:00 and noon," or "Between 2:00 and 5:00, I will talk to another adult on the phone." As the baby becomes a bit more predictable, the new mom can get more exact: "When the baby naps, I will pay those bills." Kalani's schedule, while lacking the spontaneity that her teen friends had, provided a manageable way to meet the goals she had set for herself.

Talk Kindly to Yourself

Much like Shirley and Annette, Kalani used positive self-talk to get herself through tough times, chiding herself with pep talks like "You can do this." Positive self-talk is proven to increase confidence. Everyone talks to themselves in their heads. Sometimes you boost yourself up, often you may be prone to criticize and berate yourself, looking at how everything is going wrong rather than what is going right.

Work to shush that critical part of your brain. Talk to yourself the way you might talk to a friend who was having similar anxieties. "Of course you can do this; look at the skills you have that apply here; remember how good you are with this issue." The more you can make your self-talk not only positive but specific, the more effective it will be. Rather than using a blanket "good job," tell yourself what you liked about what you did, or what evidence you have that "you can do it."

Thirteen

Separation Anxiety— The Working Mother Myth

Working Mother— Myth or Reality?

"Mothers need to be with their babies twenty-four hours a day, seven days a week, or there will be dire consequences for the baby." The facts are hotly debated every time a new study on the effects of day care is released. Many mothers fear their babies will forget them or become more attached to the day care provider. The reality is that good day care is available, and there is little that can cause a baby to forget his mother.

My name is Amanda Davis.
I'm a television news anchor and the proud
mother of a beautiful daughter.

Baby's Name: _Melora Joy_

Date of Birth: _February 20, 1984_

Time of Birth: _3:21 P.M._

Weight: _7 pounds, 4 ounces_

Length: _21 inches_

I t pained me to get Melora up from her warm crib every morning before the crack of dawn—before the sun rose to greet a new day, before the birds serenaded it with song and before she had a good night's sleep. But I had no choice. I was a single working mother trying to raise my baby and earn a living to support us. So I took Melora to a twenty-four-hour day care facility at four o'clock every weekday morning.

As an early morning television news anchor I had to report to work at four-thirty and be ready to go on the air to deliver the news at six. But

> *I was afraid Melora was going to forget about me because she wouldn't see me most of the day.*
>
> —AMANDA DAVIS

before I could think about the day's news events my first thoughts focused on my baby. I had to make sure she was safe, in the best hands and getting the best possible care while I was working. I often felt horrible about leaving Melora at day care because that meant she would spend the majority of her day with someone else loving her and holding her. Because Melora couldn't talk there was no way for her to tell me if she was being mistreated. That fact was a tremendous source of stress and pain.

Even though I was confident Melora was getting good quality care, it was also hard to leave her because we would be apart for what seemed like forever—sometimes for ten hours if I was sent out to cover a story following my anchoring duties. Those long hours of separation created my greatest fear. I was afraid Melora was going to forget about me because she wouldn't see me most of the day. I cried so much I thought my tear glands would dry up.

One thing I did to help ease my pain was take comfort in the fact that I checked out the twenty-four-hour day care center thoroughly. I visited the facility, which was located near my place of work, several times before I enrolled Melora. I talked with other parents who had children there. I wanted to make sure they were pleased with the service and that their children were happy. I also got to know the managers and talked with them extensively. In fact, I became very good friends with one of the supervisors at the day care center, and she helped keep an even closer eye on Melora.

Despite my best efforts, I wasn't insulated from an occasional problem. One day, I went to pick up my baby from the day care center. When I arrived I found her standing in a crib crying, her diaper soaking wet and the snaps on her pants undone. Melora looked as if she had not been tended to in awhile. I wondered how long she had been standing in the crib crying her eyes out wanting to be changed. That really upset me. It was far from what I expected, or wanted, to see.

I grabbed my baby and went straight to the manager to voice my concerns. At the time, Melora was still crying and I was crying, too, because I was so upset. The manager was very apologetic and assured me my daughter had not been crying all day and had, in fact, been changed several times during the day. Still, I explained that it was very disappointing and upsetting to find my baby in that condition. Receptive to my concerns, the manager assured me that situation would never happen again. And it didn't.

Finally, to help dull the pain caused by my separation anxiety, I reminded myself that Melora wouldn't be awake the entire time she was at day care. I knew she would nap several times during the day. When she wasn't asleep she would be with people who cared about her. Reflecting on my own childhood also helped get me through. I remembered my mom also worked when I was an infant. While I was left in someone else's care I don't recall a day when my mother didn't love me, care for me and spend time with me.

Having wonderful memories about the time I spent with my mother made me realize Melora would always remember me. I did the best I could to make sure she would always feel me: my love, my presence and my spirit—even in my absence. I did that by spending quality time with her after work during the week and on the weekends. When I wasn't playing with Melora, or rocking her—feeling her body next to mind—I found myself just staring at her in total amazement. She was such a little miracle and brought so much joy to my life.

I finally realized no matter how long I was separated from my baby during the day nothing could sever the ties that bind us. My belief was reaffirmed every time I picked Melora up and her face would light up the moment our eyes met. Excited, Melora would bounce uncontrollably, fling her arms toward me and wait for me to scoop her into my embrace. That small, genuine gesture told me all I needed to know.

Amanda's Savvy Strategies

- If you need to leave your child in day care, check it out thoroughly, get to know the staff, then trust your decision.
- Keep an eye on the big picture: your own memories of your mother if she worked; the cues that your child is delighted to see you each day.

Separation Anxiety—
Myths About Working Mothers

Separation anxiety is a term usually used to refer to a child having difficulty leaving a parent. But mothers suffer from it, too, as Amanda shows in her story, much like Lori did in chapter 10. Anxiety at leaving the baby is extremely common in new mothers. It does not matter whether the baby is left in day care or with family or friends, for a forty-hour work week or an afternoon at the movies. This anxiety can be quite variable, ranging from a sweet sadness and slight tearfulness to all-out sobbing and grief at having to leave the baby.

Separation anxiety is related to the growing attachment between mom and baby that was discussed in the stories of Andrea and Elizabeth. If you did not feel connected to your baby, it would not be hard to leave. As this love grows, leaving your baby often feels harder and harder. The reverse is not true, however. If you are able to leave your baby without intense emotion, it does not necessarily mean that the parent-child bond is weak. It could mean any number of things. You really are looking forward to the time away, whatever its purpose. You are secure that your baby will be safe. You are a person not given to sensitivity on such issues.

The Link Between Separation Anxiety and Bonding

A closer look at the process of parent-child bonding clarifies why separation is often troublesome to mom (or dad) and baby. Beginning during pregnancy, as the expectant mother comes to terms with this new life, the baby initially feels very much a part of her. Physically, this is the reality during pregnancy. Mom is one with the baby. She thinks of her own needs, but her needs are very closely intertwined with the needs of the baby. This was shown in chapter 10, when Lori was concerned about her food intake during pregnancy—for the baby, not just for herself.

At the birth, the physical separation begins. The new mother starts down the road to viewing her baby as a unique person apart from herself. The baby is no longer a part of her. The feeling of being one with the baby often continues in spite of being two distinct human beings. In fact, developmental theorists feel that this "oneness" is an essential part of the attachment process. Mothers must feel what their babies feel, identify and empathize with the baby's feelings, in order to feel connected to them.

Mother and baby start as one being, physically and then psychologically, and over time must progress into two. Over time, mother and baby must also recognize how they are not the same. Each must see how they have varying emotions and reactions to the world. In this way, healthy development of the relationship between them can continue. This psychological disengagement is essential in the long run, because the end goal is for children to grow up and leave home. The goal is to produce independent human beings who can go forth into the world and reproduce. And if a mother stayed as close to her baby emotionally throughout that child's life as they were during the stages of infancy, the baby would still be living at home when he was thirty-five.

It is this intense closeness, almost a sense of unity that caused Amanda to have such pain at leaving Melora at day care. Amanda may have felt like she was truly abandoning part of herself. She came in and found Melora crying, alone and wet in the crib. She was hurt because she could identify so strongly with her daughter's feelings. When our children hurt, we hurt—for them, but for ourselves, too. Amanda's frustration and concern about leaving her daughter in day care is linked to that old myth again, that mothers can protect babies 110 percent. She felt guilty, as well as angry, about the discomfort that Melora was feeling, standing in that crib crying her eyes out.

Amanda had not been able to keep her baby from all harm, even though in this case it was not life-threatening. The first time a new mother realizes that she is not omnipotent where her baby's protection is concerned is devastating. Over time, as more disappointments surface, mothers and babies survive. Each learns to deal with the everyday reality of the imperfect parent.

The Myth of Forgetting

Another issue which fueled Amanda's apprehension about child care is the idea that Melora would forget her. Several misconceptions feed into this fear, a common myth that affects new mothers. Because babies cannot communicate that they have good memories, parents often do not recognize the baby's ability to remember. Facts are helpful. Research has shown that babies can recall much from in utero: mother's voice, father's voice, music that was often played. Newborn babies will show interest in familiar sounds such as these by turning their heads toward the sound. Newborns can pick out their own mother's smell, particularly of her breast milk, over the smell of other mothers. Newborns quickly remember and recognize faces of their parents, too, preferring those familiar faces to unknown faces. If babies who are only hours or days old have such capa-

> ### Your Baby's Memory
>
> If you wish to reassure yourself that your baby will not forget you, try this experiment with your baby. When your baby is awake and alert, fed and changed, lay her on a blanket on the floor. Sit on one side, and have a friend or neighbor sit on baby's other side. Take turns saying your baby's name. Babies routinely turn their heads toward mom's voice.

bilities, certainly older babies will not forget their mothers after a day in day care, or even a week away. Mom's face, sound, smell are firmly entrenched in baby's memory. Little can disrupt this connection. Your baby knows you. Trust in that, and separation anxiety can decrease. For further information about your baby's abilities, read *Your Amazing Newborn* by Marshall and Phyllis Klaus.

Easing the Transition to Day Care

Amanda describes tools that worked for her in easing the transition to day care for both mom and baby. First of all, she was quite thorough in her "day care shopping." She checked out facilities, talked to workers and parents, observed how babies were cared for. Amanda made a special effort to get to know teachers and administrators personally. When you are a real person to the staff, your baby will be more than a number also.

Leaving your baby may be fraught with emotion. You will feel more satisfied with your choice if you use all your rational powers to check it out and evaluate the options. Lori's struggle to leave her baby in day care, described in chapter 10, was eased by starting slowly. If possible, it is extremely helpful to begin leaving your baby at the chosen facility in small doses before you return to work. Follow these guidelines:

- Let the baby stay for only two hours the first day.
- Stay four hours the next day, but stay with your baby for half that time.
- Gradually increase the amount of time the baby stays while you are gone.

This can help both baby and mother feel much more relaxed. Alternatively, you may want to start back to work on a part-time basis for a week or so. Then slowly add hours as you both ease into the new routine. If you need to take it slowly like this, know that nothing is the matter with you. Good day care facilities will foster this adjustment process rather than be bothered by it. If the setting you have selected is not cooperative in this way, you may want to step back and reevaluate your choice.

Understand Your Baby's Cues

Finally, Amanda ultimately found that her fears about Melora's forgetting her were relieved when she began to read her baby's cues. Certainly, once your child can communicate verbally, you will find it easier to leave her because then she can tell you what happened in your absence. But as Amanda discovered, Melora portrayed a great deal to her mother with her body language. Melora's face lit up, and she would literally throw herself in her mother's direction at the end of the day.

Reading your child's physical cues can tell you not only that he is glad to see you, but how comfortable he is in the day care setting. Children who are being well cared for will seem happy and relaxed with their caregivers even while sad to let go of the parent dropping them off. Brief crying and clinging are inevitable for most children at one time or another. This usually does not signal a serious problem unless the unhappiness persists for most of the day. Wise parents will take into account a child's natural swings in anxiety about being left.

Leave-Taking Varies with Age and Ability

Separation anxiety waxes and wanes according to the developmental stage of the child. One of the most well-known times of anxiety comes at approximately eight months of age. This is when babies can truly recognize that mom is not part of them. As discussed above, a mother's separation anxiety depends on that connection and oneness with her child. Likewise, the

Experiencing an increase in separation problems? Ask yourself these questions:
- Is your child at a new stage in development?
- Has something changed in another part of your child's life?
- Has there been a change at the day care facility?
- Has your child been moved to a new class?
- Did a favorite teacher quit?

baby's anxiety will rise dramatically when he begins to realize that he and mom are not one and the same. Then it dawns on him: If he and mom are not the same person, then she could disappear and not return!

With this newly found knowledge, he may crawl after her as she leaves the room. If baby is not yet mobile, he may cry if mom so much as ducks into the bathroom for a quiet moment. When a child is in day care at this age, separation on a daily basis is often filled with great amounts of anguish for both mom and baby. As your child grows and continually broadens his ability to think, he will certainly go through more stages like this. Leaving him gets to be a true ordeal again for awhile. If your child has suddenly increased his crying as you leave him at day care, this is the most likely explanation.

Consulting a good developmental guidebook or your child's pediatrician will often ease your mind about the normalcy of this new development. When children enter these times of increased anxiety about leaving parents, you can smooth the rough spots. Spend a little extra time with your child at the facility before you leave for work. Listening to your child's cues, and trusting your instincts as well as the staff at the facility, should enable you to ride out the situation, making changes as necessary.

Fourteen

Turning Point—
The Job of Mother
Myth

The Job of Mother—
Myth or Reality?

Once again, societal myths paint a glowing picture of what the job of mothering is like. Our culture leads you to believe that being a mother is fun, rewarding and endlessly productive. The realities of the job are often at odds with your pre-baby expectations. The job is repetitive, physical, isolated, demanding. The rewards are many—but not very evident in the first weeks of your child's life.

My name is Ruthanne Kern.
I am a stay-at-home mom and the proud
mother of identical twin girls.

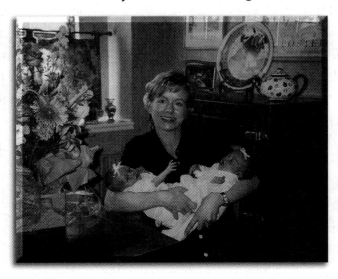

Baby's Name: *MacKenzie*

Date of Birth: *Oct. 15, 1999*

Time of Birth: *7:41 P.M.*

Weight: *7 pounds, 4 ounces*

Length: *19 ½ inches*

Baby's Name: *Lauren*

Date of Birth: *Oct. 15, 1999*

Time of Birth: *7:46 P.M.*

Weight: *5 pounds, 9 ounces*

Length: *18 ¾ inches*

I am probably the happiest mother on the face of the Earth, but I didn't always feel that way. There were times when I thought I was losing my mind, times when I longed for normalcy, but didn't recognize what normal was, and times when I longed to be in another place and time. Not anymore. I feel happy, complete and satisfied where I am. It took me a long time to reach this point in my life. But the important thing is: I made it.

In December of 1999, I was at the top of my game, the "go to" person, the team captain. I was working as a high-powered sales exec at an advertising agency. I absolutely loved my career—thrived on the stress, the fast pace and the intensity that were par for the course in that high-stakes industry. While my husband and I had talked about starting a family, I decided to put off having a baby and forge ahead with my career. I wanted to see how high up I could go in the company.

There were times when I thought I was losing my mind, times when I longed for normalcy, but didn't recognize what normal was, and times when I longed to be in another place and time.

—RUTHANNE KERN

Before the Christmas holidays, I interviewed for a management position at my agency. I had no doubts about getting the promotion. I just knew the job was mine. I was absolutely certain of it. After a fabulous time celebrating Christmas and

New Year's I returned to work anxious to find out when I would start my new position. My first day back I was sitting at my desk when the telephone rang. I hoped the caller on the line was my boss. Nervous, I removed the receiver from its cradle and blurted a greeting into its mouthpiece.

I sighed and thought to myself: *This is it, the call that is going to rocket my career to new heights.* Excited, I listened closely as my boss began to speak. He made small talk about the holidays and then in a very matter of fact tone told me I did not get the promotion. The company had decided to hire a woman I was very good friends with, but who worked in another office. I was shocked and couldn't believe my ears. I felt I had earned the promotion—worked long and hard for it. I was devastated. Not getting the management position was the most severe blow I had ever received in my career.

Reeling from the pain of defeat, I tried to assess my career and plan my next course of action. Because my husband and I had agreed if I did not get the new job we would go ahead and start a family, I figured that option into my strategy. It took me about a month to get over the professional setback and to get a grip on myself and my life again. After careful consideration, my husband and I decided it was a good time for us to have a baby. We had been married five years. We had worked hard, and we had achieved success.

Much to my surprise, I conceived quickly. My husband took me away on a ski trip in March during spring break. I was just exhausted every night and starving every day. I didn't know what was wrong. It wasn't until we returned home from vacation that it occurred to me that I must be pregnant. When my doctor confirmed my suspicions, I felt excited, scared and thrilled all at the same time.

When I went back to work, I was afraid to share my wonderful news with my colleagues. It was like I had this really cool secret, but I couldn't tell anybody. I wanted to make sure everything was going well with my pregnancy first. So I went about my business as usual: making calls, checking accounts and scheduling appointments. The ringing of the telephone suddenly interrupted my routine. It was my doctor. She phoned to tell me a high level of hormones had been detected in my bloodstream. That could mean multiple births. When I hung up I merely sat at my desk unable to speak. Stunned, I tried to absorb the news—multiple births?

The possibility of twins was puzzling to me. Neither my husband nor I have a history of twins in our family. We were not taking fertility drugs. So it never entered my mind that I could be carrying twins. The notion of multiple births was rather ironic because my husband and I had decided we only wanted to have one child. Even though I agreed to that decision, it was difficult for me to accept it and be at peace with it because I come from a large family—I couldn't see having just one baby.

A couple of days later, a sonogram revealed my two babies on a small monitor. When I caught a glimpse of their images on the small screen I was overwhelmed with emotion. I realized they were a true blessing from God because he knew deep in my heart I wanted to have more than one child. So he gave me one pregnancy with two babies. My husband and I were grateful and couldn't wait for our little ones to arrive.

Because of my petite size and light weight, my doctor warned me there was no way I would be able to work throughout the full term of my pregnancy. She suggested that at some point I would have to go on bed rest. As the weeks progressed, I was determined to continue to work. I felt fine. I wasn't sick at all. I was just hungry all the time, and a little tired. However, it wasn't long before I started having high blood pressure, nosebleeds and swelling feet—warning signs to slow down and take it easy.

During a weekly examination in July, my doctor advised me to tell my superiors I had to go on bed rest. It was a difficult thing for me to talk with them about. I felt like I was leaving my family. I felt sorry and guilty for having to go. In fact, I cried when I told my boss I was taking time off. I just didn't want to quit my job, not for a second, but I did. I stayed home. I lounged around in big T-shirts and maternity shorts while stretched out on the couch with my feet up. I was bored and frustrated. Going from working in an intense, stressful, fast-paced environment to coming home and sitting around idly was an enormous adjustment for me.

It didn't take long before I began to feel less useful. I had always felt like I had a strong sense of purpose with my life and with my job. I would get up, go to work and feel like my colleagues really needed me. I loved that. But then I found myself sitting at home reading books and putting pictures in photo albums while the office continued to function without me. That's when I began to realize my whole life was changing—the place I had carved out in the world for myself was turning 180 degrees.

My body was changing, too. I gained forty-four pounds. My stomach began to expand over my hips. Everything started to protrude out. I had one baby head up, and the other baby head down. They were head-to-toe on either end. I couldn't get off the couch, my feet were swollen, I was uncomfortable and I didn't feel attractive at all. That caused me to cut back on going out socially. My husband and friends kept telling me how great I looked, but my own personal hang-ups prevented me from believing them.

I wanted to be this well-put-together, well-dressed person, with a thriving career. Instead, I was sitting at home, gaining weight, not doing anything and not going out. I felt bad because virtually all of my friends expected me to be happy and excited—especially about having twins—but I wasn't. I wasn't happy because I couldn't get up and prepare for my babies, I felt like crying all the time and everything was a big ordeal. I began to wallow in the lowest depths of misery.

Feeling my babies move around inside of me did wonders for my spirit. That awesome experience pulled me out of a land of misery and thrust me into a land of miracles. I was so amazed, I no longer felt uncomfortable and unattractive, but rather euphoric. That incredible feeling washed away those dark moments from my memory. Just knowing my babies were growing inside of me was an absolute miracle. To think my body was capable of producing not one but two babies was powerfully astounding. The whole experience of giving birth gave me a profound sense of appreciation for human beings—especially my babies.

When I looked at their beautiful faces I could not believe I gave birth to them. I was so excited and thrilled by the extraordinary experience. I think I cried for two weeks straight—every day, twenty-four hours a day, literally. I think some of the tears were brought on by exhaustion. I was so tired. When my husband and I brought Lauren and MacKenzie home, I was just overwhelmed. My husband was a huge help to me and very supportive during my pregnancy, but he was extremely busy with work after the babies were born.

We brought our twins home on a Sunday afternoon in October. Monday morning my husband—who works out of our home—went into his office, picked up the phone, shut the door and went to work. He left me standing on the other side of the door looking at our two babies thinking, *What do I do now?* I didn't have a clue. I wondered why there wasn't someone with me to tell me what to do. I was so lost I didn't even know who to call for help.

I found doing basic care for my twins an extremely challenging task. Because I believed breastfeeding was going to be their best chance for staying as healthy as they could, for as long as they could, I was determined to do it. I put both of the girls on the same schedule and fed them at the same time. When I didn't follow that routine, I was feeding one, putting her down, feeding the other and putting her down, and by the time I did that the other one was up and wanting to eat again. I wasn't getting any time for myself or getting any breaks.

The alternative proved to be just as exhausting. Nursing both of the girls at the same time was very tiring and totally uncomfortable for me and for them. I did not enjoy breast-feeding at all. In fact, one day my husband came in the room when I was nursing and I had tears streaming down my face. With his voice swelling with emotion, he said, "This has got to end. If it's not any good for you, it can't possibly be that good for the babies." My husband made it clear that my mental and physical health were more important than what I was going through.

Putting the girls on bottles was a big help. Other people could help me feed them and that made an enormous difference in my life. However, between feeding, burping, changing diapers and bathing the twins, I was running on empty all the time. I was supposed to be eating right, resting and taking care of myself, but I wasn't doing any of that—not at all. I didn't have time.

My babies and I were on this rapidly moving frustrating cycle. It got to a point where I was just going through the motions of what I had to do as a mom. I didn't feel like I was spending any time just holding and loving my babies. That made me sad and angry. I had read books about mothers gazing into their babies' eyes and the babies cooing and cuddling up next to their moms, and I looked forward to that experience. But I didn't have any of that. I just felt like a machine doing one thing after another. And I felt like my babies were suffering emotionally because of it.

The few times I had a break from Lauren and MacKenzie,

I felt like I was attached to them at the hip. Everything I was doing revolved around them: picking up after them, washing their clothes, buying their food. I felt like I was suffocating. I needed some time for myself—just to sit down and catch my breath. Yet, at the same time, I longed to spend time with my girls doing things other than "mommy" things. Like taking them with me to have lunch with a girlfriend or going shopping.

The few times I managed to take my babies out in public I noticed other moms and how easy they seemed to have it. I would see moms with one baby, and they'd stop the car, take the baby out of the infant car seat, put her into a stroller, and off they would go—happy-go-lucky. I felt envious. The moms would look so put together, and they would be laughing and smiling at their one baby. Whereas I spent so much time changing the girls, getting them dressed, putting them in their car seats, putting all of their stuff in the car, and then driving to our destination—I was exhausted.

When we arrived at our destination, I had to do everything again in reverse: take out their strollers, take the babies out of their infant car seats, strap the babies into the strollers, take out their stuff. By the time I did all that and got to where we were going I would have wasted so much time that there wouldn't be enough left to have lunch with a friend or do any shopping. It was just too much work. I felt very overwhelmed. But, I couldn't tell anyone I wasn't "loving" motherhood because everyone assumes that you are. My friends were calling me and saying, "Gosh, I envy you. You get to stay at home with your babies. You're so lucky." I was lucky, but I was not happy.

I felt like I had been dropped into a place where I didn't belong. There were times when I would sit in the nursery with my girls, and they would be on the floor playing with their toys, gurgling, and doing the things babies do, and I would just sit there and cry my eyes out. Mostly, out of sadness for myself. I thought to myself: *I have everything—more than I ever dreamed of in my life—a wonderful family, a wonderful home and a husband who supports me staying home, and yet I feel so sad.* All I wanted to do was go back to work.

I wanted to be in a place where I knew everything, where everybody came to me for answers to tough questions, and where I was the one who had everything together. I felt alone at home because my husband traveled Monday through Friday and only came home on weekends. Everyone else in my extended family worked full time so they could not come over during the week. And I didn't have all the answers about how to care for my babies.

By August I felt like I was absolutely going to lose my mind. I had not had a break away from my girls. I had not been anywhere socially. I had not done anything except care for my babies. Realizing I needed a vacation, my husband said, "Let's go away for the weekend." The grandmothers came and stayed with the girls. I typed them seven pages of notes on the twins' routine—even though we were only going to be gone for two nights. I was looking forward to the trip, but even while away I felt like I could not manage. I could not function. I had this dismal feeling all the time. I didn't understand it.

I remember telling my OB/GYN how I felt, and she seemed to think it was just my hormones trying to get back into a normal pattern, because they had gotten so out of whack when I was pregnant. She suggested it would take a little longer for them to settle down because I had twins. So my doctor kept saying, "This is normal." But I wasn't getting any better emotionally. I found it very hard to manage.

I kept thinking, *This is not the way my life is supposed to be. I'm not enjoying my babies. I'm not enjoying my life.* I felt bad about that. I figured something must be wrong with me. Around this time, my husband got new insurance and I called and set up an appointment with a brand-new doctor—someone I didn't know and who I had picked at random from a list of doctors on our medical plan. The moment I met my new doctor I knew I could trust her and open up to her. I don't know why I felt that way—it was just a strong vibe I got from her.

After a thorough examination, I sat down and told my new doctor about the way I felt. She said, "This is not normal." Then she gave me a questionnaire to fill out and some literature about postpartum depression (PPD) to read. On my next visit, my doctor diagnosed me with severe depression and suggested I consider taking an antidepressant. In a way, I was relieved because it said to me, "There is something wrong with you. You are not losing your mind."

I had always viewed depression as something mental you

could just pull yourself out of—like talking yourself out of a
bad day. I also saw it as a sign of weakness, like you were not
capable of handling life. In my case, I was not capable of handling motherhood—my twins. That really hurt me and made
me feel unsure and inadequate.

I left the doctor's office and headed home straight to my
computer. I conducted a lot of research on PPD on the
Internet. I also gathered brochures on women's health from
my local pharmacy. I tried to come to terms with being
depressed. The way I came to grips with it was to accept the
fact that depression is an illness. It's an illness like diabetes or
high blood pressure or anything else. And sometimes, it takes
medicine to control it.

During my next visit with my new doctor, we talked extensively about depression—what causes it and how best to treat
it. When my doctor told me an antidepressant would make me
feel normal again, I just looked at her and cried because at
that point in my life I was very sad and confused. Through
warm tears, I looked at her and said, "I don't know what normal is. How am I supposed to recognize it?"

When I left my doctor's office I took a prescription and her
promise to monitor me closely to heart. The hardest part of
the ordeal was going home and telling my husband what was
happening. It is a difficult thing to tell someone else—
especially your husband—that you're not capable of taking
care of babies, your own babies. And if you're going to have
to do it, you've got to take medicine. I really didn't know how
to explain that to him and make myself look good in the

process. But I knew I had to be open and honest with my husband about what I was going through.

As it turned out, my husband was relieved because he had noticed the drastic changes in me. He knew I was not myself. He knew I was not happy. He knew we were constantly at odds with each other. He knew all of those things. As hard as it was for me to open up and share my feelings, it proved to be the best thing I ever did, because it also helped my husband understand something was really wrong with me.

After being on the medication for about a week I finally started to feel normal again. I recognized it. And it felt good. I felt happy and free of the longing to go back in time, to go back to a place that was totally familiar. I was free of the layers of negative feelings that gripped me: sadness, depression, anger and confusion. I was ready to move full speed ahead into my new world.

My biggest fear, however, was that I would have to take antidepressants for the rest of my life. My doctor explained that if that's what it took for me to cope and keep the chemicals in my brain balanced then that's what we would do. She also made it clear, however, that most people taking antidepressants reach a point where they no longer need the medicine to function. Then they are weaned off of it. That's what happened to me. I was weaned off the medicine gradually. I stopped taking it about a year later.

I am so grateful I found a doctor who understood what I was going through and could help me get better. In retrospect, I realize having a baby—in my case, twins—leaving a job I was successful at and loved, and staying home were major life changes that were overwhelming and contributed to my depression. When I think about whether I was caring for my babies in my darkest hour, I realize I was. I was lavishing them with love. I was feeding them. I was changing them. I was caring for them.

I get goose bumps a lot now—especially when I see my girls' cute little smiles or when I witness funny things or special things they do. Like when they walk over and give each other kisses just because. And when they run up to me, throw their arms around my neck, and give me big hugs and kisses out of the blue. It is the best—the absolute best. I feel so much happiness and joy now. Overwhelming joy. I am thankful that I am home with my daughters. I cherish every second we spend together. I'm enjoying motherhood. I'm enjoying my new life. I am at a point where I wouldn't trade what I have for anything—not even the highest-paying job in the world!

Ruthanne's Savvy Strategies

1. Persistence until she found a health-care provider who understood her depression and validated her feelings.
2. Her ability to recognize her triumphs even through her darkest moments—that she loved and cared for her babies in spite of her depression.

Turning Point—
The Job of Mother Myth

Postpartum depression (PPD) strikes approximately 10 to 20 percent of new mothers in this country. Ruthanne's story paints a realistic picture of what happens for many women. It explores the role of a woman's life situation, psychological makeup and biochemical influences in bringing her to this painful point. Ruthanne had tremendous changes in her life. She had to switch from a high-powered businesswoman, focusing on tangible outcomes and profits, to an expectant mother on bed rest. Being pregnant and actually imagining the outcome is tough.

What a woman on bed rest is doing is very intangible. She often feels simply like a human incubator. She cannot anticipate her baby in any of the usual, visible ways, like preparing the room or accumulating the layette. She must just sit and wait. Most women on bed rest have similar feelings of uselessness, even if they are not executives. For a woman like Ruthanne, accustomed to seeing the concrete results of her efforts, this must have seemed nearly unbearable.

The Myth of Blissful Pregnancy

Ruthanne was facing the myth of "blissful pregnancy," just as Terri did in chapter 10. Pregnancy is falsely believed to be universally wonderful. Our culture expects women to be "glowing" and "radiating happiness." Renaissance paintings of a tranquil, though obviously pregnant Madonna, firmly place this image in most expectant mothers' minds. These images, whether from classical paintings or current magazines, give little clue to the physical discomfort Ruthanne was enduring. Swollen ankles, swollen abdomen and backaches make it hard to feel serene.

Most pregnant women have mood swings, weight gain, fatigue. All of these symptoms are also signs of depression, making it difficult to detect during pregnancy. The facts indicate that women are just as likely to be depressed during pregnancy as at any other time in their lives. The hormones of pregnancy do not offer protection from bad moods, and the bodily changes can bring genuine aches and pains.

Ruthanne was caught in the direct crossfire of the old "how wonderful" expectations of her friends and family, and the realities of physical distress and boredom. She was happy to have twins, but she felt completely worn down physically. When you are anticipating a calm, blissful nine months, the reality can be downright discouraging, as it was for Ruthanne. She became quite disheartened.

This illustrates one of the first risk factors for PPD: prenatal mood. If a woman has suffered depression or anxiety at another point in her life, particularly during pregnancy, her risk for PPD is greater than for women who have never had such extreme emotional swings. When the babies began to move and so seemed more real, Ruthanne's wait did get a bit easier. Feeling the babies move inside of her helped her perceive the importance of bed rest to the end goal: healthy babies. Then her mood improved.

Social Support and PPD

After the babies were born, Ruthanne ran up against another risk factor for postpartum depression: lack of social support. She was so alone when her husband closed the door and went back to work in his office. She had no help. She had two babies to feed, diaper and soothe. Taking care of one baby alone can be overwhelming. Two babies certainly double the load. It is no small wonder that Ruthanne felt like she was running on empty. It sounds like she was. She was caring for two babies all alone.

This meant breaks, difficult to squeeze into the day in the best circumstances, became absolutely impossible. Ruthanne slipped into autopilot mode. She had to operate like a machine in order to meet her babies' most basic needs. Because her "old self" had gotten things done with great skill, she hung in there. Ruthanne felt like she was a failure because this was not easy. She wished to return to work, when everyone else was telling her how lucky she was. All she wanted was a life she could control like she was used to, rather than one which controlled her.

Ruthanne did not receive much validation. No one said, "Of course it is hard—you must be exhausted taking care of two babies." Her physician did not even offer this reassurance. The doctor rather discounted her struggles as a hormonal imbalance that would even out with time. This may have been because of Ruthanne's previous accomplishments. Her family and friends saw her as a person who could always handle every situation. They expected she would manage this with flying colors as well. Nor did she receive much practical help, probably for the same reason. Imagine her friends saying "Ruthanne? Why, she can do anything—she'll be fine."

Most women with PPD are so ashamed that this picture-perfect, greeting-card existence they imagined hasn't materialized that they blame themselves. *There must be something the matter with me,* they think. This isn't how I imagined it. Everyone else seems to be having a good time except me. Ruthanne remarks on how she watched mothers of single babies breezing right along into the mall to have lunch with friends. How could it be so easy for them when this simple task seemed insurmountable to her?

Myths About the Job of Mother

In Ruthanne's mind, part of the problem was her inability to produce. Her efforts to get out and have lunch, packing both babies up, hauling them out, hoisting them into the stroller, all seemed like a "waste of time." She could not cross her accomplishments off in her day planner. Her daily tasks were never complete. But these events are not a waste of time. They are simply part of life with a baby. Compared to how she used to measure time, though, it does seem unproductive.

Many women fall prey to this myth about the job of mother. If everyone is telling you that motherhood is a wonderful thing, then certainly the job will feel ideal from day one. The job must be glamorous and fulfilling, with changes every day as your child flourishes. Then the day-to-day reality sets in.

Motherhood seems to be an unending round of bodily fluid cleaning, crying, lifting, pacing. The rewards are few and far between. It is hard to feel productive. New mothers often get stuck in this negative cycle. They cannot see what is beneficial about the repetitive, time-consuming tasks of motherhood.

The Status of Mothers

As a culture, the status accorded to motherhood is part of this problem in valuing the job of mothering. Because it is an unpaid, untrained position, motherhood seems to fall into the category of unskilled and unimportant as well. The women in Jane Weaver and Jane Ussher's study were quite outspoken about this lack of status accorded to the job of mothering. They described the syndrome as "just a mother." Mothers are viewed negatively, dismissed, devalued and blamed for unruly children. Mothers are perceived as people without much intelligence and without a past. Any previous (or current) standing does not seem to matter.

> ### Mother Prejudice
>
> You may have experienced this phenomenon, as I did at a party. I was obviously pregnant with my first child. After being introduced to a woman I did not know, she asked "When are you due?" I answered. There was a slight pause, as she turned away, scanning the room for someone else to talk with. And then she left! If I was a mother, I must be only a mother, and not have any other interesting facets worth getting to know.
>
> —ANN DUNNEWOLD, PH.D.

The persona of "mother" seems to engulf your identity, wiping out your previous value. Women may impose these beliefs upon themselves as Ruthanne did, feeling worthless except to their children. Because of our "product-oriented" culture, Ruthanne was blinded to the very important contribution she was making by caring for her babies. Baby care is certainly not a waste of time.

Social Support from Other Mothers

Many women feel better about the value of mothering when they socialize with other mothers. Because Ruthanne did not have much social support, she had no help in beating this cultural prejudice. The women in Jane Weaver and Jane Ussher's study reported that they had status only within the circle of other mothers, not within society as a whole. Ruthanne might have seen more clearly the value of her endless efforts with her babies if she had other mothers around to remind her.

Postpartum Depression and Mothering

Ruthanne looks back and reflects on her depression now that she feels better. She acknowledges that even in the midst of her worst negative emotions she was still able to love and care for her babies. She was doing a critical job for the success of the human race as well as individually for her children. For women suffering from postpartum depression, this accomplishment is common but nevertheless praiseworthy.

When you are feeling as badly as Ruthanne did, you find little joy or interest in your life. You may be crying frequently and feeling like a worthless failure. It is often hard to complete anything. But research shows that repeatedly women with overwhelming depression still manage to care for their children. And they care for them effectively. Many new mothers with PPD report being able to "rally" for the baby. They may not be able to even smile for their partner, but they can still sing a lullaby or evoke a giggle out of their baby. This ability prevents the PPD from having a long-term effect on the infant.

Another risk factor for PPD is marital conflict or discontent. Preexisting conflict certainly makes the postpartum adjustment difficult for the couple. The old adage that "babies don't fix marriages" is true. If conflict can be addressed before the baby arrives, the couple has a much greater chance of making a smooth transition to this new stage in their family life. Couples must face how to handle the baby and this new way of life together. They must come to terms with a shift in focus from each other to the baby as the center of attention.

Then there is the reality of less time together. Either partner may feel displaced by the other's attention to the new baby. The sexual relationship is often affected as well, as was shown in Casey's story. If these problems are not easily resolved or if the couple has other lingering relationship resentments, PPD often is the end result.

Resentment in the Marriage

Ruthanne and her husband did not appear to have conflicts before the babies arrived. But their experience after the babies were born is representative of many new parents. Their story illustrates clearly how conflict can arise in the couple even when the relationship was smooth before parenting. When

Ruthanne's husband went into his office and closed the door, he seemed to say that there were aspects of his life that were not going to change. The impact of becoming a parent differs for men versus women, according to Anne Woollett and Mel Parr. Even in these days of equality, men are often less involved. So the changes in the new father's life may be less substantial or less abrupt than the changes in the new mother's life. Men are often able to keep the parenting and other preexisting roles more distinct. Ruthanne's husband closing the door, leaving her with the babies, could not have been more symbolic of this fact.

Ruthanne seemed to feel simply lost at this contrast. Her life was altered irrevocably while her husband's life rocked on with minor adjustments. Many new mothers react with anger at this disparity. "How can he sit there in the recliner, holding the baby and saying how his life has not really changed, when my world has been turned upside down?" laments many a new mother. And this anger grows if there is not an effort to balance the change for each partner. Anger is a significant part of PPD for many sufferers. Increasing the fairness in their daily lives can decrease the anger.

Depletion Depression

Part of Ruthanne's exhaustion stemmed from no real break from October until August. On any other demanding job, your supervisor would be pushing you to have a break after ten months without a single holiday or weekend off. Parenting is no different. No one can be expected to work 168 hours a week nonstop. Breaks must provide relief when they are scheduled. It does not help to use break time to perform simply another aspect of the job of parenting. Ruthanne seemed to use what few breaks she had to run household errands, rather than engage in some fun. It is no surprise that she became even more depressed and discouraged with her role as mom. She was totally depleted, running on empty.

When someone is under stress for an extended period of time like Ruthanne, it is not uncommon for the stress to eventually take a toll on the new mother's body. Stress hormones at high levels in the body influence the chemical balance in a woman's brain. This can result in the need for medication. The second physician Ruthanne consulted understood this reality. She gave Ruthanne's symptoms a name. This is often the first step to feeling better. This was the validation that Ruthanne needed all along. She was not weak, a failure or a person who made a mistake and wrecked her life. She simply had a physical illness. This doctor helped Ruthanne see that the need for an antidepressant was not a sign of her weakness, but rather a result of a chemical imbalance.

PPD is a real disease, not a failure for the new mother. Antidepressants can be incredibly helpful in allowing a new mother to sleep, to think more clearly, to lift the cloud of worry, anger or depression that shrouds her life. These medications enable the new mother to feel like herself again. They are not a "happy pill" or magic fix. The problems in her life will not simply disappear but will seem more manageable. She may still need to resolve marital issues. She might require a change in her work situation. With the help of the medication, she may now be able to solve these issues more effectively or quickly. Psychoactive drugs are not always necessary for treatment of postpartum depression. Psychotherapy, diet and exercise, social support from friends or peer support groups, all have a role in aiding the new mother's recovery.

Identifying Postpartum Depression

Since approximately 80 percent of new mothers have some negative feelings, many women wonder how to distinguish serious PPD from the ups and downs of normal adjustment. The answer is quite simple. If at any point the new mother feels like the bad feelings outweigh the good feelings in her life, she may be experiencing PPD. Normal adjustment, by comparison, means the new mom has

> ### How Partners Can Help
>
> New mothers need to have their partners take charge of specific responsibilities for the baby, such as the evening bath, the last feeding or keeping diapers stocked.
>
> Partners need to make sure that the new mom has time off from her duties every evening and every weekend.

more good days than bad days, more happy moments than sad ones. Like Ruthanne, if you find that you have lost interest in normal activities and find no joy in your life, you are probably enduring PPD. See chapter 15 for more information on recognizing the symptoms and risk factors for postpartum depression, and on locating help in your area.

Grieving Postpartum Depression

Finally, Ruthanne encountered a loss common to women who have had postpartum depression. She grieved that her first year with her new babies was so miserable. Even when feeling better, many moms who have had PPD feel continued sadness about that lost time. There may be memory gaps for the good times. Images of crying or panic attacks may be their primary recollections of the immediate postpartum weeks. It is essential to allow the new mom time to feel this regret in order to move forward. If you have had PPD, you may feel fully recovered only when you can finish this mourning for that missing postpartum bliss. So take the time to feel the sadness. Work to balance the bad memories with the good, and cherish the joys at each small triumph in the present and in days to come.

> **You may need medical or psychological help if:**
>
> 1. Daily activities such as eating, dressing, taking care of the baby or sleeping are affected
> 2. Worries about the baby or imagined harm to self or others exist
> 3. Efforts to feel better, such as going on an outing, are unsuccessful
> 4. Support sources are worn out, either in providing help or by listening

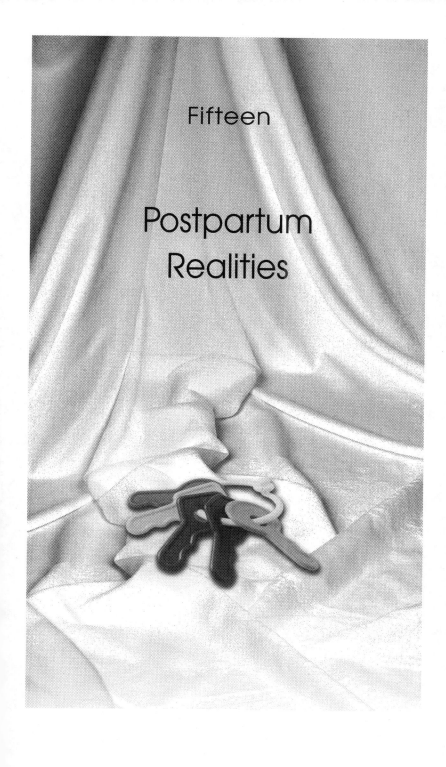

Fifteen

Postpartum Realities

L oss of sleep is an essential adjustment to becoming a parent. If the sleep disruption in your life has taken its toll, the following tips for coping with insomnia might aid in the retraining of your body clock. This is necessary to again achieve a reasonable night's sleep:

1. Keep to a regular sleep/wake cycle by going to bed and getting up at the same time each day.
2. Have a bedtime routine: a bath, a sleep-inducing snack, relaxing to music.
3. Reserve the bed for only sleep and sleep-related activities. Do not pay bills in bed or allow yourself to lie awake for long periods. Your body will learn to associate the bed with being awake, rather than asleep.
4. Exercise early in the day. An eight-minute walk can boost your mood and help you sleep, but may keep you awake if done in the evening.

5. Consider creative sleep arrangements: Take the baby to bed if that works for you; trade off with your spouse on night feedings, with the parent on duty sleeping in the room with the baby so the other parent can have distance from the baby's cries.

6. Don't lose sleep over losing sleep. Focus on deep breathing and relaxing, allowing sleep to come rather than chasing after it. Arrange to decrease demands the next day if you have a particularly bad night—take the baby to bed with you for the day while you try to catch up.

Symptoms of Postpartum Depression

While postpartum depression (PPD) is the name given to the collection of symptoms a new mother may have after the birth of her baby, the idea of "depression" is often a misnomer. Many more new mothers feel intense anxiety, irritability and anger rather than tearfulness and low mood. The following list of symptoms shows just how variable and changing a new mother's emotions can be:

- Anger
- Appetite changes
- Confusion
- Crying
- Delusions
- Distractibility
- Lethargy
- Loneliness
- Loss of interest
- Mood swings
- Numbness
- Panic attacks

- Dizziness
- Fatigue
- Feelings of failure
- Hallucinations
- Headaches
- Irritability

- Restlessness
- Self-doubt
- Shame
- Sleeplessness
- Stomachaches
- Worry

The new mother may vacillate between any of these symptoms. She certainly has good days mixed in with the bad days. This leads her to believe that she will be able to conquer this. When her mood swings in another direction the next day, she may feel very discouraged. This is simply how postpartum depression progresses.

RISK FACTORS FOR PPD

Some of the risk factors for PPD were addressed in Ruthanne's story in chapter 14. Here is a checklist of the common risk factors:

- Another child under two years of age or multiple children under five years of age
- Biological vulnerability: thyroid problems, PMS, infertility, chronic fatigue, fibromyalgia
- Birth complications and/or previous pregnancy loss
- Depression or anxiety during pregnancy
- Financial stresses

- Lack of confidence, personally or as a parent
- Lack of social support
- Life stresses such as a move, job change, family illness
- Loss, either recently or early in life
- Marital conflict or discontent
- Negative thinking patterns/pessimism
- Perfectionism, expectations of control in your life
- Personal or family history of depression, anxiety or related conditions
- Problems with the baby: medical issues, colic, high-need or fussy temperament
- Single parenting

If you have even one of these risk factors, your chance of experiencing PPD is greater than average. Knowing what to expect, how to care for yourself physically and/or emotionally, and identifying sources of social, medical and psychological support are all important to minimize the effects of PPD on your life when you become a parent.

If you are seeking help for PPD, talk to your health care provider or childbirth educator about local resources. The following organizations may be helpful in identifying knowledgeable mental health providers, telephone contact volunteers or support groups in your area:

Postpartum Support International
927 N. Kellogg Avenue
Santa Barbara, CA 93111
(805) 967-7636
www.postpartum.net

Depression After Delivery—National
91 E. Somerset St.
Raritan, NJ 08869
(800) 944-4773 (4PPD)
www.depressionafterdelivery.com

For more information, the following books are excellent resources:

Dunnewold, Ann and D. Sanford. *Postpartum Survival Guide.* Oakland, CA: New Harbinger Publications, 1994. Out of print, but may still be available from the author. Please call 214-343-1353.

Huysman, Arlene. *A Mother's Tears: Understanding the Mood Swings that Follow Childbirth.* New York: Seven Stories Press, 1998.

Osmond, Marie, Marcia Wilkie and Judith Moore. *Behind the Smile: My Journey Out of Postpartum Depression.* New York: Warner Books, 2001.

Placksin, Sally. *Mothering the New Mother: Your Postpartum Resource Companion.* New York: Newmarket Press, 2000.

Raskin, Valerie. *When Words Are Not Enough: The Women's Prescription for Depression and Anxiety.* New York: Broadway Books, 1997.

Afterword

A FINAL LOOK—
DR. DUNNEWOLD

The brave mothers who share their stories in these pages help untangle the mystery of what becoming a mother is like. As A. Oakley says in *Becoming a Mother* (1979), "Becoming a mother is a journey into the unknown." Thanks to the members of the Motherhood Club, it need not be so scary. What these stories make clear is that, again and again, becoming a mother is a growth process. It is not instantaneous, occurring magically in some moment. Rather, it is travel along an arduous path, a journey that takes time.

These women move from embracing societal myths about what mothering will be like to defining their own way to fit that role. They progress from believing they can protect their children perfectly and that their children are fragile and require this protection, to an acceptance that the child is resilient with skills of his own. These mothers move from a connection to only the idea of this new person, to a full-blown, person-to-person commitment and love for the new child's uniqueness.

Their attitudes are transformed from a "me" focus to a "mom mentality" with all the sacrifice that entails. At the beginning, these moms buy into the impossible-to-fulfill "perfect mother" myth. Through the day-to-day muck and hard work, they realize this goal will never be met. They let go and recognize that they can do a "good enough" job loving and teaching their children anyway. Like the mothers in the study by Jane Weaver and Jane Ussher, these women discovered that this pilgrimage through motherhood is chock-full of positives and negatives.

The negative aspect was most often attributed to the practical issues of exhaustion, loss of freedom and time constraints. Conversely, the emotional aspects were universally positive, rich with joy at the love and pride they felt for their babies. Finally, these women share how they preserved their previous sense of themselves as women, even while they learned to love the often exhausting, draining, confusing and challenging role of mother.

How did these women get through this maze of motherhood?

- They learned to take care of themselves physically. All mothers must allow time for rest, for exercise and for healthy eating. It is just as important for a mother as for her growing child.
- They nurtured themselves emotionally. They connected

with their partners, with loved ones, with old friends and new. They took time for fun. They fostered the "non-mom" parts of themselves.

- They talked in a kindly and encouraging manner to themselves.
- When they felt discouraged or confused they consulted experts, either other mothers or medical professionals.
- They trusted in themselves.

You can manage these steps, one by one. When you do, you will feel the same triumph expressed throughout this book by the members of the Motherhood Club.

Epilogue

I have been deeply moved by these magnificent mothers and their extraordinary stories. As I talked with them and remembered my own challenges, I began to get a greater understanding of how they embrace the realities of mothering. I also realize how much mothers give of themselves as they settle into motherhood—the most important role they will ever have. And how willingly they love, nurture and care for their babies without expecting celebration—although richly deserved. So, as you embrace your greatest role, know you will feel a wealth of emotions along the way—some negative and some positive. Rest assured, however, that the positives almost always outweigh the negatives.

As you travel the path of motherhood, talk about your feelings and reactions to mothering. Don't be afraid to express how you feel whether it is happiness or sadness. Being honest with yourself and others about mothering is a freeing experience, and it will allow you to enjoy all motherhood has to offer: its profound joy, miracles and magic.

I hope you realize mothering is a wonderful experience that sometimes brings misery in various forms, including guilt, frustration and confusion. Some of that is triggered by a lack of mothering skills. Don't worry. You will develop them. When you do, the misery that grips you will release you and you will soar. As your spirit rises higher and higher, your trials will become a distant memory that will only serve to educate you, free you of self-condemnation and strengthen the bond you share with your baby.

I also hope you have gained knowledge, strength and encouragement from the women in the Motherhood Club. They opened their hearts and shared their wisdom, honesty and experience with mothering. Who could ask for anything more? There is so much to be learned from their invaluable lessons, from the research and from Dr. Ann Dunnewold's powerful clinical analysis, which helps us better understand the emotional, physical and psychological side of mothering.

If you cross the threshold where you find mothering too overwhelming to bear and you need to talk with another mother, do it. If you need to take a break from mothering, do it. If the inherent feelings that go along with mothering urge you to contact a professional for help, do it. You'll be extremely glad you did.

Always remember, when members of the Motherhood Club tell you that "You are a good mother," believe them. When they tell you that "mothering gets better," believe them. And when they tell you mothering is the most extraordinary experience you will ever have, believe them. Then, release a sigh, relax and reap the rewards derived from being a mother—and proud member of the Motherhood Club!

P.S. I would love to hear about your experience as you settled into motherhood. Please send your success story to:

The Motherhood Club
P.O. Box 540244
Grand Prairie, Texas 75054-0244
Or e-mail me at *Shirley@TheMotherhoodClub.com*

Appendix

L
isted below is more information about the research
studies in this book.

Beck, Cheryl Tatano (1992). The lived experience of postpartum depression: a phenomenological study. *Nursing
Research,* 41:166–170.

Beck, Cheryl Tatano (1993). Teetering on the edge: A sub-
stantive theory of postpartum depression. *Nursing
Research,* 42:42–48.

Dr. Beck is a professor of nursing at the University of
Connecticut and a certified nurse midwife. In these two studies, she interviewed nineteen women who were suffering
from postpartum depression. From the interviews, she discovered consistent themes which plague women in the adjustment to parenthood.

Bloch, Miki, Schmidt, Peter, Danaceau, Merry, Murphy, Jean, Nieman, Lynnette, & Rubinow, David. (2000). Role of falling hormone levels in postpartum depression. *American Journal of Psychiatry,* 157:924–930.

These researchers, who are physicians and nurses, studied two groups of women, eight with prior postpartum depression and eight with no such history. Women were given hormones to replicate the high levels of postpartum hormones, and then these hormones were eliminated in their systems. Women with a previous history of depression became depressed, while those without that history did not.

Brown, S., Small, R., & Lumley, J. (1997). Being a "good mother." *Journal of Reproductive and Infant Psychology,* 15:185-200.

These researchers interviewed ninety women at the Centre for the Study of Mothers' and Childrens' Health in Victoria, Australia in 1989 on a broad range of issues related to the experience of motherhood in the first two years. This paper focuses on the women's conceptions of a "good mother." Women who had been depressed and women with no history of depression had similar views about what makes a "good mother."

Oakley, A. (1980). *Women Confined: Towards a Sociology of Childbirth.* Oxford: Martin Robertson.

This book addresses societal pressures that influence women's ideas about motherhood.

Redshaw, M. E. (1997). Mothers of babies requiring special care: attitudes and experiences. *Journal of Reproductive and Infant Psychology,* 15:109–120.

This psychologist distributed questionnaires to 420 families who had babies in 23 neonatal units in England. She studied the factors they found stressful about having their babies in specialized neonatal care.

Weaver, J. J., & Ussher, J. M. (1997). How motherhood changes life—a discourse analytic study with mothers of young children. *Journal of Reproductive and Infant Psychology,* 15:51–68.

These psychology researchers interviewed thirteen mothers with children between the ages of one and three about the changes in their lives as a result of becoming parents. They identified six themes which were repeated in the interviews, and the societal myths which affected the women's perceptions.

Woollett, A., & Parr, M. (1997). Psychological tasks for women and men in the postpartum. *Journal of Reproductive and Infant Psychology,* 15:159–184.

These researchers from the University of East London Psychology Department studied 106 men's and 106 women's responses to becoming parents over the course of the first year.

Organizations That Support Mothers

Depression After Delivery, Inc.
91 E. Somerset St.
Raritan, NJ 08869
(800) 944-4773 (4PPD)
www.depressionafterdelivery.com

Depression After Delivery, Inc. offers information and referral on postpartum depression and related disorders. Knowledgeable professionals, telephone peer support and support group listings are available.

Family Support America
20 N. Wacker Dr., Suite 1100
Chicago, IL 60606
(312) 338-0900
www.familysupportamerica.org

Family Support America is an alliance dedicated to helping families. It also provides information about locating and starting family support organizations in your area.

La Leche League International
1400 N. Meacham Road
Schaumberg, IL 60168-4079
800 La Leche (800-525-3243) or (847) 519-7730
www.lalecheleague.org

La Leche League International is dedicated to providing information and support to encourage breastfeeding. Listings are available for support groups in your area.

National Association of Mothers' Centers
64 Division
Levittown, NY 11710
(516) 520-2929 or (800) 645-3828
www.motherscenter.org

The National Association of Mothers' Centers offers referrals to a center in your area where you can receive support, parent training and related information. If a center does not exist near you and you wish to start one, they can provide advice on that process.

National Organization of Mothers of Twins
P.O. Box 438
Thompson Station, TN 37179-0438
(615) 595-0936
(877) 540-2200

The National Organization of Mothers of Twins offers support to mothers of multiples. It also offers referrals for a club in your area.

Parents as Teachers National Center
10176 Corporate Square Drive
St. Louis. MO 63132
(314) 432-4330

Parents as Teachers programs are based on the philosophy that parents are a child's first and best teachers. This national clearinghouse provides information on locating or starting a Parent as Teachers program in your area, based on an established curriculum.

Postpartum Support International
927 N. Kellogg Avenue
Santa Barbara, CA 93111
(805) 967-7636
www.postpartum.net

Postpartum Support International provides information about postpartum emotional disorders and referral to resources such as mental health professionals or support groups in your area. Training for health professionals is also provided.

Besides providing much valuable information to new mothers, these organizations offer many links to additional resources from their Web sites.

Recommended Reading for New Mothers

Postpartum Depression

Dunnewold, Ann and Diane Sanford. *Postpartum Survival Guide.** Oakland, Calif: New Harbinger Publications, 1994.

Huysman, Arlene. *A Mother's Tears: Understanding the Mood Swings That Follow Childbirth.* New York: Seven Stories Press, 1998.

Osmond, Marie, Marcia Wilkie and Judith Moor. *Behind the Smile: My Journey Out of Postpartum Depression.* New York: Warner Books, 2001.

Placksin, Sally. *Mothering the New Mother: Your Postpartum Resource Companion,* New York: Newmarket Press, 2000.

Raskin, Valerie. *When Words Are Not Enough. The Women's Prescriptions for Depression and Anxiety.* New York: Broadway Books, 1997.

---

*Out of print, but may be available from the author. Please call 214-343-1353.

Resources About Babies

Brazelton, T. Berry and Stanley Greenspan. *The Irreducible Needs of Children: What Every Child Must Have to Flourish.* Cambridge, Mass: Perseus, 2000.

Brazelton, T. Berry. *Touchpoints: Your Child's Emotional and Behavioral Development.* New York: Addison-Wesley, 1992.

Gerber, Magda. *Dear Parent: Caring for Infants with Respect.* Los Angeles: Resources for Infant Educators, 1998.

Gerber, Magda and Allison Johnson. *Your Self-Confident Baby.* New York: John Wiley & Sons. Inc., 1998.

Klaus, Marshall and Phyllis Klaus. *Your Amazing Newborn,* Cambridge, Mass.: Perseus, 1998.

Babies, Crying and Sleep

Ferber, Richard. *Solve Your Child's Sleep Problems.* New York: Fireside Books, 1985.

Jones, Sandy. *Crying Baby, Sleepless Nights.* Boston: Harvard Common Press, 1992.

Sammons, William. *The Self-Calmed Baby.* Boston: Little, Brown, 1989.

Taubman, Bruce. *Why Is My Baby Crying?* Harrisburg, Penn.: White Hat Communications, 2000.

Resources on Breastfeeding

Huggins, Kathleen. *The Nursing Mother's Companion.* Boston: Harvard Common Press, 1999.

Pryor, Gale. *Nursing Mother, Working Mother.* Boston: Harvard Common Press, 1997.

Parenting Strategies

Faber, Adele and Elaine Mazlish. *How to Talk So Kids Will Listen and Listen So Kids Will Talk.* New York: Avon Books, 1999.

_____ . *Siblings Without Rivalry.* New York: Avon Books, 1998.

Wyckoff, Jerry. *Discipline Without Shouting or Spanking.* Deephaven, Minn.: Meadowbrook Books, 1984.

Silver, Nan. *Rules for Parents: Simple Strategies That Help Little Kids Thrive and You Survive.* New York: Berkley Books, 2000.

The Couple Relationship

Godek, Gregory J. P. *1001 Ways to Be Romantic.* Naperville, Ill.: Casablanca Press, 1995.

Gottman, John and Joan DeClaire. *The Relationship Cure.* New York: Crown Publishers, 2001.

Coping with Motherhood Through Humor

Einhorn, Amy. *The Fourth Trimester: And You Thought Labor Was Hard: Advice, Humor, and Inspiration for New Moms on Surviving the First Six Weeks and Beyond.* New York: Crown, 2001.

Shelton, Sandi Kahn. *Sleeping Through the Night and Other Lies: Mysteries, Marvel, and Mayhem in the First Three Years of Parenthood.* New York: St. Martin's Press, 1999.

_____ . *You Might As Well Laugh: Surviving the Joys of Parenthood.* Baltimore: Bancroft Press, 1997.

About the Authors

Shirley Washington is married and the mother of a beautiful little boy. A native of St. Louis, Missouri, Shirley graduated from Southern Illinois University at Carbondale with a degree in broadcast journalism. Shirley is a television news anchor/reporter at KDFW-TV in Dallas, Texas. She has won numerous awards for journalism excellence, including the prestigious Emmy and Alfred P. Murrow Award for breaking news coverage. Shirley has worked at television stations in Atlanta, Nashville, Des Moines, Moline, Illinois, and Decatur, Illinois. She lives in the Dallas area with her husband and son.

Ann Dunnewold, Ph.D., is a licensed psychologist in independent practice in Dallas, Texas, specializing in emotional aspects of reproductive function, such as prenatal and postpartum depression, PMS, pregnancy loss, infertility and menopause. Dr. Dunnewold is active nationally in educating professionals and the public on issues surrounding the transition to parenthood. She is coauthor of *Postpartum Survival Guide* (New Harbinger Publications, 1994) and author of several works on postpartum issues for medical professionals. A mother of two daughters, Dr. Dunnewold found her own initiation into the Motherhood Club to be incredibly life-altering—just like mothers everywhere.

Celebrate Motherhood